LIVING ANIMALS OF THE BIBLE

אַ לְדָוִ֗ד ...

2 אַשְׂכִּ֨ילָה ׀ בְּדֶ֬רֶךְ תָּמִ֗ים מָ...

3 לְבָבִ֥י בְּקֶ֥רֶב בֵּיתִ֑י לֹא־אָשִׁ֓ית ׀ לְ...

4 עֲשֹֽׂה־סֵטִ֥ים שָׂנֵ֗אתִי לֹ֣א יִדְבַּ֣ק בִּ֑י לֵבָ֓ב ...

ה רָ֭ע לֹ֣א אֵדָ֑ע׃ מְלָשְׁנִ֬י בַסֵּ֨תֶר ׀ רֵעֵ֗הוּ אוֹת֬וֹ אַצְמִ֥ית גְּ...

6 עֵינַ֤י ׀ וּרְחַב־לֵ֭בָב אֹת֗וֹ לֹ֣א אוּכָ֑ל׃ עֵינַ֤י ׀ בְּנֶאֶמְנֵי־אֶ֗רֶץ

7 לָשֶׁ֣בֶת עִמָּדִ֑י הֹ֭לֵךְ בְּדֶ֣רֶךְ תָּמִ֗ים ה֤וּא יְשָׁרְתֵ֥נִי׃ לֹא־יֵשֵׁ֨ב ׀

בְּקֶ֬רֶב בֵּיתִי֮ עֹשֵׂ֪ה רְמִיָּ֫ה דֹּבֵ֥ר שְׁקָרִ֑ים לֹא־יִכּ֗וֹן לְנֶ֣גֶד עֵינָֽי׃

8 לַבְּקָרִ֗ים אַצְמִ֥ית כָּל־רִשְׁעֵי־אָ֑רֶץ לְהַכְרִ֥ית מֵעִיר־יְ֝הֹוָ֗ה כָּל־פֹּ֥עֲלֵי אָֽוֶן׃

PSAL. CII. קב

2 תְּפִלָּ֗ה לְעָנִ֥י כִֽי־יַעֲטֹ֑ף וְלִפְנֵ֥י יְ֝הֹוָ֗ה יִשְׁפֹּ֥ךְ שִׂיחֽוֹ׃ יְהֹוָ֗ה

3 שִׁמְעָ֥ה תְפִלָּתִ֑י וְ֝שַׁוְעָתִ֗י אֵלֶ֥יךָ תָבֽוֹא׃ אַל־תַּסְתֵּ֬ר ׀ פָּנֶ֨יךָ ׀

מִמֶּנִּי֮ בְּי֢וֹם צַ֫רִי־לִ֥י הַטֵּֽה־אֵלַ֥י אׇזְנֶ֑ךָ בְּי֥וֹם אֶ֝קְרָ֗א מַהֵ֥ר עֲנֵֽנִי׃

4 כִּֽי־כָל֣וּ בְעָשָׁ֣ן יָמָ֑י וְ֝עַצְמוֹתַ֗י כְּמוֹ־קֵ֥ד נִחָֽרוּ׃ ה הוּכָּ֖ה כָעֵ֥שֶׂב

6 וַיִּבַ֣שׁ לִבִּ֑י כִּֽי־שָׁ֝כַ֗חְתִּי מֵאֲכֹ֥ל לַחְמִֽי׃ מִקּ֥וֹל אַנְחָתִ֑י דָּבְקָ֖ה

7 עַצְמִ֣י לִבְשָׂרִֽי׃ דָּ֭מִיתִי לִקְאַ֣ת מִדְבָּ֑ר הָ֝יִ֗יתִי כְּכ֥וֹס חֳרָבֽוֹת׃

9 שָׁקַ֥דְתִּי וָאֶהְיֶ֑ה כְּ֝צִפּ֗וֹר בּוֹדֵ֥ד עַל־גָּֽג׃ כָּל־הַ֭יּוֹם חֵרְפ֣וּנִי

י אוֹיְבָ֑י מְ֝הוֹלָלַ֗י בִּ֣י נִשְׁבָּֽעוּ׃ כִּי־אֵ֭פֶר כַּלֶּ֣חֶם אָכָ֑לְתִּי וְשִׁקֻּוַ֥י

11 בִּבְכִ֥י מָסָֽכְתִּי׃ מִפְּנֵי־זַֽעַמְךָ֥ וְקִצְפֶּ֑ךָ כִּ֥י נְ֝שָׂאתַ֗נִי וַתַּשְׁלִיכֵֽנִי׃ יָמַ֗י

PSALM CII.

A Prayer of the afflicted, when he is overwhelmed, and poureth out his complaint before the LORD.

HEAR my prayer, O LORD, and let my cry come unto thee.

2 Hide not thy face from me in the day when I am in trouble; incline thine ear unto me: in the day when I call answer me speedily.

3 For my days are consumed like smoke, and my bones are burned as an hearth.

4 My heart is smitten, and withered like grass; so that I forget to eat my bread.

5 By reason of the voice of my groaning my bones cleave to my skin.

6 I am like a pelican of the wilderness: I am like an owl of the desert.

7 I watch, and am as a sparrow alone upon the house top.

8 Mine enemies reproach me all the day; and they that are mad against me are sworn against me.

9 For I have eaten ashes like bread, and mingled my drink with weeping.

10 Because of thine indignation and thy wrath: for thou hast lifted me up, and cast me down.

11 My days are like a shadow that declineth: and I am withered like grass.

(fragment, Psalm CI)

...ill

...faith...

...may dwell

...in a perfect

...worketh deceit shall not

...my house: he that telleth

...t tarry in my sight.

...early destroy all the wicked

...the land; that I may cut off all wicked doers from the city of the LORD.

LIVING ANIMALS

OF THE BIBLE

Text and Illustrations by

WALTER W. FERGUSON

Charles Scribner's Sons • New York

FRONTISPIECE: Nubian ibex

1 3 5 7 9 11 13 15 17 19 x/p 20 18 16 14 12 10 8 6 4 2

Library of Congress Catalog Card Number 72–11112
SBN 684–13346–6 (cloth)

Manufactured in Israel by Nateev ltd.

CONTENTS

PREFACE

In organizing the material in this book, the biblical Hebrew name of the animal is given first, using the Sephardic transliteration. The most likely English common name follows, then the nearest approximation to the scientific name—species or subspecies, genus, family, or order. Animals are listed in the index under biblical Hebrew names and English common names. The Hebrew names do not of course apply to New Testament references.

Biblical quotations in the text follow the Authorized (King James) Version unless otherwise noted. In certain cases, the Revised Standard Version or the Anchor Bible supplies a more accurate reading and has therefore been used.

As a measurement of time the form B.C.E. (Before the Common Era) has been used in place of B.C., to which it is equivalent.

Grateful acknowledgment for editorial assistance is made to Dr. George M. Landes, Baldwin Professor of Sacred Literature, Union Theological Seminary; Dr. Walter A. Fairservis, Jr., professor and chairman of the Department of Anthropology and Sociology, Vassar College, and acting curator of the Eurasian Anthropology Collections, American Museum of Natural History; and Robert F. Scott, Associate Editorial Director, Professional and Technical Programs, Inc. Special thanks are also due to Mrs. Judith Finck for editorial assistance and for typing the manuscript.

INTRODUCTION

> And out of the ground the Lord God formed every beast of
> the field, and every fowl of the air; and brought them unto
> Adam to see what he would call them: and whatsoever Adam
> called every living creature, that was the name thereof (Genesis 2:19).

The Bible is in a way one of the earliest books touching upon animal lore.
About one hundred animals are mentioned in the Old Testament alone.
Domestic animals were regarded mainly in terms of food, transportation, and
sacrifice, and wild animals with varying degrees of interest, sympathy, and
fear. There were laws outlining which species were or were not to be eaten,
how they were to be bred, cared for, and slaughtered. Animals were used in
parables and figures of speech to enlighten or admonish the populace. In
many instances the only existing evidence describing the animals that inhabited
the Holy Land thousands of years ago, some of which have since become
extinct, is found in the Scriptures.

The original translators and commentators were theologians and their
knowledge of zoology and paleontology was limited. A number of lists of
Bible animals have been compiled and these range from the erudite to the
absurd. From the English translation, several books and articles dealing
with Bible animals were published, illustrated partly with species that lived
in England and even in America, rather than in the Holy Land. I have
tried to re-examine the identification in the light of present knowledge of
local species, whether living, extinct, or extirpated.

In some cases it is possible to identify with certainty not only the
species but even the subspecies involved—for example the Syrian races of
the bear and ostrich. Animals that were of particular importance, such as
the goat, were given names distinguishing the gender and age. Animals of
lesser importance were often lumped under generic terms that defined a
whole family, such as mice, or a whole order, such as bats. A name such as
'achashterānîm, which appears only twice (Esther 8:10,14) and seems to have
no Hebrew root, was probably borrowed from some other language, in this
case Persian. Many names are open to question or virtually impossible to

pin down and have been given translations pulled out of thin air. The justification for the determination of the te'ô as the Arabian oryx is scant indeed, and in the case of the qippōd the ambiguity is hopeless. Certain names may have originally been applied to imaginary beasts or monsters. Some animals were imported from other areas, along with their native names, and foreign names were sometimes applied to local animals. And just as some animals today have more than one common name and one name may apply to more than one species, so it may be that leviathan (livyātān) at one time meant crocodile, at another time whale, and sometimes sea monster.

In many instances, speculation is probably futile, but I have not been able to resist the temptation to offer my opinion. I have contented myself with the nearest reasonable name I can arrive at, whether generic or specific, and as a last resort have used the original Hebrew name.

LIVING ANIMALS OF THE BIBLE

BEZOAR

MAMMALS

qōf (*pl.*, **qōfîm**)
ape, monkey
Cercopithecidae

The word qōfîm appears only in a verse which occurs in approximately the same form in two books of the Old Testament.

> For the king had at sea a navy of Tharshish, with the navy of Hiram;
> once in three years came the navy of Tharshish, bringing gold, and silver,
> ivory, and apes, and peacocks (I Kings 10:22; see also II Chronicles 9:21).

It seems reasonable to assume that the apes or monkeys were brought from the same area as the other goods mentioned. This is likely to have been the East African coast, since Hiram's fleet also traded with Ophir (I Kings 10:11) in the region of Somaliland and Solomon brought horses from Egypt (I Kings 10:28). The word qōf is Egyptian in origin (as is tukkîyyîm, which also occurs in this passage; see tukkî). Ceylon and India have also been suggested as the trading area.

RHESUS MONKEY AND SACRED BABOON

EGYPTIAN FRUIT BAT

'atallef (*pl.*, 'atallēfîm)

bat

Chiroptera

In the Old Testament bats are included among "unclean" birds and also among "creepers on all fours."

> And the stork, the heron after her kind, and the hoopoe, and the bat (Leviticus 11:19; see also Deuteronomy 14:18).

In Isaiah's prophecy of the coming of the Lord's kingdom:

> In that day a man shall cast his idols of silver, and his idols of gold, which they made each one for himself to worship, to the moles [mole-rats] and to the bats (Isaiah 2:20).

As many as twenty-five species of bats have been recorded from the Holy Land, but all are lumped together under the single generic name 'atallēfîm. The most conspicuous species are the Egyptian fruit bat, *Pteropus aegyptiacus*, and Kuhl's pipistrelle, *Pipistrellus kuhli*.

kelev
dog
Canis familiaris

No individual breeds of dogs are mentioned in the Bible. The references to dogs often concern their usefulness (or lack of it) in tending sheep and guarding the house:

> But now they that are younger than I have me in derision, whose fathers I would have disdained to set with the dogs of my flock (Job 30:1).

> His watchmen are blind: they are all ignorant, they are all dumb dogs, they cannot bark; sleeping, lying down, loving to slumber (Isaiah 56:10).

A comparison with a gazelle was flattering, but a comparison with a dog was derogatory:

> Yea, they are greedy dogs which can never have enough (Isaiah 56:11).

As many as five types of pariah dogs have been described from Israel. After Palestine became a British Mandate in 1923 they were largely exterminated by an antirabies campaign, but some, such as the short-haired saluki, are kept by the Bedouin, and the Canaan is being bred.

SALUKI

ze'ēv

wolf

Canis lupus

WOLF

Some of the earliest prejudices against the wolf appear in the Scriptures. There are many allusions to its ferocity:

> Benjamin shall raven as a wolf; in the morning he shall devour the prey, and at night he shall divide the spoil (Genesis 49:27).

> Beware of false prophets, which come to you in sheep's clothing, but inwardly they are ravening wolves (Matthew 7:15).

When attacking sheep and lambs, wolves are compared to cruel persecutors:

> Behold I send you forth as sheep in the midst of wolves . . . (Matthew 10:16).

> Go your ways: behold, I sent you forth as lambs among wolves (Luke 10:3).

> Her princes in the midst thereof are like wolves ravening the prey, to shed blood, and to destroy souls, to get dishonest gain (Ezekiel 22:27).

> . . . an hireling, and not the shepherd . . . seeth the wolf coming . . . and fleeth; and the wolf catcheth them and scattereth the sheep (John 10:12).

Noting its nocturnal habits:

> . . . her judges are evening wolves; they gnaw not the bones till the morrow (Zephaniah 3:3).

The wolf in Israel is represented by the Indian race which penetrates the country from the north in the winter, and the smaller Arabian race which is resident in the desert. It is usually solitary, although three or four have been seen together. Although wolves occasionally kill sheep or goats, they are useful as scavengers. The official attitude, if not the individual one, has certainly changed since biblical times, and Israel today is one of the few countries in which wolves are protected.

tan (*pl.*, **tannîm**)
Syrian jackal
Canis aureus syriaca

Tan is sometimes translated as dragon, but the jackal is intended. Perhaps because of the animal's gregarious habits, it usually appears in the plural form tannîm, sometimes confused with tannîn, singular, sometimes translated as sea monster (see tannîn). The animal's mournful cry was noted:

> For this I will lament and wail; I will go stripped and naked; I will make lamentation like the jackals . . . (Micah 1:8; Revised Standard Version).

Its habitat was also described:

> Thorns shall grow over its strongholds, nettles and thistles in its fortresses. It shall be the haunt of jackals . . . (Isaiah 34:13; Revised Standard Version).

Until a few years ago, a wild chorus of jackals could be heard in Israel on moonlit nights. Now, except for the sounds of the highway, the night is still. The jackal was once very common throughout the country up to the edge of the desert, but as a result of rabies control it has practically disappeared.

SYRIAN JACKAL

PALESTINE FOX

shû'āl

fox

Vulpes vulpes

The word shû'āl undoubtedly refers to the fox, with one possible exception:

> And Samson went and caught three hundred foxes, and took firebrands, and turned tail to tail, and put a firebrand in the midst between two tails (Judges 15:4).

It would have been easier to capture such a large number of jackals, which travel in packs, than of foxes, which are solitary.

Many habits typical of the fox were noticed:

> Catch us the foxes, the little foxes, that spoil the vineyards, for our vineyards are in blossom (Song of Solomon 2:15; Revised Standard Version).

> Now Tobiah the Ammonite . . . said, Even that which they build, if a fox go up, he shall even break down their stone wall (Nehemiah 4:3).

> And Jesus saith unto him, The foxes have holes, and the birds of the air have nests; but the Son of man hath not where to lay his head (Matthew 8:20).

The fox, although not numerous, is perhaps the most common and widespread predator in the region.

dōv

Syrian bear

Ursus arctos syriacus

SYRIAN BEAR

The bear of the Bible was undoubtedly the Syrian bear, a paler race of the Eurasian brown bear. In biblical times the bear was a menace to vineyards and to sheep and goats.

> But David said to Saul, Your servant used to keep sheep for his father, and when there came a lion, or a bear, and took a lamb from the flock, I went after him, and smote him, and delivered it out of his mouth; and if he arose against me, I caught him by his beard, and smote him, and killed him (I Samuel 17:34-35; Revised Standard Version).

A mother bear separated from her cubs is used as an analogy to advise Absalom:

> . . . thou knowest thy father and his men, that they be mighty men, and they be chafed in their minds, as a bear robbed of her whelps in the field . . . (II Samuel 17:8).

16

The ferocity of the bear is further shown in the story about Elisha:

> And he went up from thence unto Beth-el: . . . there came forth little
> children out of the city, and mocked him and said unto him, Go up,
> thou bald head; go up, thou bald head.
> And he turned back . . . and cursed them in the name of the Lord.
> And there came forth two she bears out of the wood, and tare forty
> and two children of them (II Kings 2:23,24).

The Syrian bear has disappeared from the Holy Land within the last century.

ʻayit

striped hyena (*Hyaena hyaena syriaca*) (?),
bird of prey (?)

The word ʻayit is translated as fowl in the Authorized Version
and as bird of prey in the Revised Standard Version and the
Anchor Bible. One reference indicates that it is a scavenger:

> And when the fowls [ʻayit] came down upon the
> carcases, Abram drove them away (Genesis 15:11).

ʻAyit tsāvuaʻ has been translated as speckled bird.

STRIPED HYENA

> Does my heritage remind me of a speckled bird of
> prey . . . (Jeremiah 12:9; Anchor Bible).

The ʻayit does not appear in the list of unclean birds. Since it is a scavenger and since all
inedible birds are listed there, it may well be a mammal.

Inedible mammals are not all listed—the prerequisites make this unnecessary. The references
could describe an animal that is a scavenger of striking markings, and the hyena has been suggested.
The modern Hebrew word for the striped hyena is tsāvuaʻ. It is a scavenger, usually eating offal but
also known to exhume bodies. Its teeth and jaws are so powerful that they can easily crack the bones
of an ox. Although it shirks contact with man, it is regarded with horror and fear. In Israel it was
formerly common throughout the country but in recent years has grown scarce in the north, probably
as a result of poisoning. It is strictly protected.

'arî, 'aryeh, layish, lāvî', shachal, kefîr (young lion), gûr (cub)
lion
Panthera leo

The lion appears often in the Scriptures; in fact, the numerous biblical references are the only evidence that it existed in Israel. It was used as a symbol for the princely tribe of Judah. The lion is described as the most powerful, daring, and impressive of all carnivores, and as having a terrifying roar.

> A lion which is strongest among beasts, and turneth not away for any (Proverbs 30:30).
>
> . . . they shall roar like young lions: yea, they shall roar, and lay hold of the prey, and shall carry it away safe . . . (Isaiah 5:29).
>
> The lion hath roared, who will not fear? (Amos 3:8).
>
> Then went Samson down, and his father and his mother, to Timnath, and came to the vineyards of Timnath: and, behold, a young lion roared against him.
> . . . and he rent him as he would have rent a kid, and he had nothing in his hand . . . (Judges 14:5-6).

The lion's ferocity made it an appropriate metaphor for a fierce and malignant enemy:

> Save me from the lion's mouth . . . (Psalms 22:21).
>
> . . . and I was delivered out of the mouth of the lion (II Timothy 4:17).
>
> . . . The Lord that delivered me out of the paw of the lion . . . (I Samuel 17:37).

Driven by hunger, the lion ventured to attack flocks in the presence of the shepherd:

> For thus hath the Lord spoken unto me, Like as the lion and the young lion roaring on his prey, when a multitude of shepherds is called forth against him, he will not be afraid of their voice, nor abase himself for the noise of them . . . (Isaiah 31:4).

As a youth, David killed both lions and bears when they attacked his father's flock (I Samuel 17:34-35; quoted under dōv).

LION

The habits and habitats of the lion are described:

Wilt thou hunt the prey for the lion? or fill the appetite of the young lions,
When they couch in their dens, and abide in the covert to lie in wait? (Job 38:39,40).

Behold, like a lion coming up from the jungle of the Jordan . . . (Jeremiah 49:19;
Revised Standard Version).

The well-known story of Daniel's being cast into the lion's den is in Daniel 6:16-23. And the often-quoted hope for messianic peace includes the lines:

. . . and the calf and the young lion and the fatling [shall dwell] together . . . (Isaiah 11:6).

CHEETAH

LEOPARD

nāmēr

leopard, cheetah

Panthera pardus, Acinonyx jubatus

The word nāmēr occurs several times and seems to describe the leopard.

> Can the Ethiopian change his skin, or the leopard his spots? (Jeremiah 13:23).

The leopard was feared because of his terrible strength.

> . . . a leopard shall watch over their cities; everyone that goeth out thence shall be torn in pieces . . . (Jeremiah 5:6).

The prophets foretold that in the time of the messiah:

> . . . the leopard shall lie down with the kid . . . (Isaiah 11:6).

The hilly regions of Lebanon seem to have been frequented by leopards in ancient times:

> Come with me from Lebanon, my spouse, with me from Lebanon: look from the top of Amana, from the top of Shenir and Hermon, from the lions' dens, from the mountains of the leopards (Song of Solomon 4:8).

The oracle describing the threat of the Chaldeans states:

> Their horses also are swifter than the leopards . . . (Habbakuk 1:8).

In this last reference the cheetah, rather than the leopard, may have been intended. The cursorial cheetah, sometimes trained for hunting, apparently became extinct in the area during the past century.

The leopard has the widest distribution of any cat. Although it is in danger of extirpation, it still survives in the wilderness in Israel and is strictly protected.

shāfān

rock hyrax, coney

Procavia capensis syriaca

The shāfān of the Bible is the rock hyrax, not the hare with which it has been confused because of a superficial resemblance in size and color. The hyrax has short ears and well-developed canines, and all its toes have nails except for the innermost hind toe which bears a claw. It was erroneously considered a ruminant on account of the way it moves its jaw when eating but nevertheless was among the animals forbidden as food under Mosaic law because it was not hoofed.

> And the coney, because he cheweth the cud, but divideth not the hoof;
> he is unclean unto you (Leviticus 11:5).

Hyraxes are found throughout Israel wherever there are rocky mountains (Psalms 104:18). They find protection by inhabiting holes and crevices on steep and often inaccessible hillsides, where they can be seen sprawled out taking a sun bath or jumping nimbly from rock to rock.

> The conies are but a feeble folk, yet make they their houses in the rocks
> (Proverbs 30:26).

ROCK HYRAX

sûs, rekesh

horse

Equus caballus orientalis

Sûs is commonly used for horse in the Old Testament, but rekesh also occurs. Rekesh is sometimes translated in the Authorized Version as mule but in later versions as horse; it means horse in modern Hebrew (see pered). Horses appear many times in the Bible. They seem to have been domesticated from 4000 to 2000 B.C.E. in the steppes of the Ukraine, and about 1700 B.C.E. horse-drawn chariots were used throughout the Middle East. Horses were already present in Canaan when the Hebrews first arrived. Since they do not "part the hoof" or "chew the cud," they were not included among animals permitted to be eaten.

During the patriarchal age, long after their settlement of Canaan, the Hebrews were a pastoral people and had little need for horses. Horse-drawn chariots were used in idolatrous processions:

> And he took away the horses that the kings of Judah had given to the sun . . . (II Kings 23:11).

There was an injunction against kings' breeding horses:

> But he shall not multiply horses to himself, nor cause the people to return to Egypt, to the end that he should multiply horses . . . (Deuteronomy 17:16).

Delivering the post on horseback dates far back:

> . . . and sealed it with the king's ring, and sent letters by posts on horseback . . . (Esther 8:10).

Comparisons with horses are not very complimentary:

> Be ye not as the horse, or as the mule . . . whose mouth must be held in with bit and bridle . . . (Psalms 32:9).

> A whip for the horse, a bridle for the ass, and a rod for the fool's back (Proverbs 26:3).

The thoroughbred Arabian horse is characterized by its small stature and concave nasal profile. Pure breeds are rare today. In Israel horses are decreasing in importance and numbers.

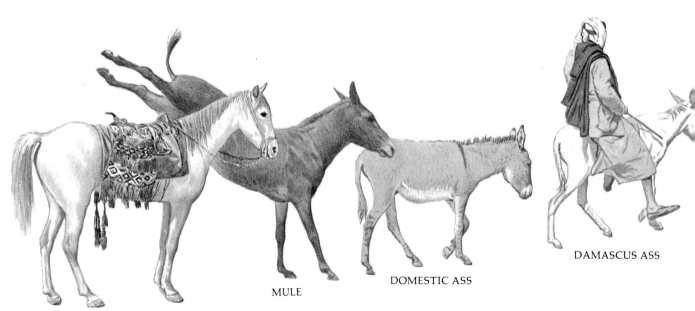

ARABIAN HORSE

MULE

DOMESTIC ASS

DAMASCUS ASS

pered
mule

Equus caballus + *Equus asinus*

Mules, which are the hybrid offspring of a male ass and a female horse, were not used by the Hebrews until the time of King David; at that time mules and horses replaced asses as royal beasts. Since hybridization was forbidden by Mosaic law (Leviticus 19:19), mules were probably imported from Egypt. In David's time and later, the mule was used as a riding animal:

> The king also said unto them, Take with you the servants of your lord, and cause Solomon my son to ride upon mine own mule, and bring him down to Gihon (I Kings 1:33).

The mule is also mentioned as a beast of burden (II Kings 5:17). It was valued for its strength, being able to carry greater weight and having more power of endurance in mountainous country than the horse, ass, or camel. Although much less important today, mules are still used in Israel.

The word rekesh is also sometimes translated as mule in the Authorized Version but not in later versions (see rekesh).

chamôr, 'atôn (female), 'ayir (young)
domestic ass or donkey

Equus asinus domesticus

The domestic ass is frequently mentioned in the Bible. It was an important animal and was used for agriculture (Deuteronomy 22:10), as a beast of burden (I Samuel 16:20), and for riding (Genesis 22:3). When the Hebrews returned from the Babylonian exile, they brought back six thousand, seven hundred and twenty asses (Ezra 2:67). The domestic ass or donkey was probably descended from the wild ass of northeast Africa (*Equus asinus*). It was probably domesticated on the shores of the Mediterranean or in the Nile Valley and was found in Egypt before the horse. Although the domestic breeds have changed much in color, some still reveal ancestral markings, such as the shoulder stripe of the Nubian race or the barred legs of the Somali race. The ass has been known in Israel only since biblical times, and a large white breed, known today as the Damascus ass, was apparently even then highly esteemed as a riding animal:

> Speak, ye that ride on white asses . . . (Judges 5:10)

The domestic ass was protected by legal restrictions, along with the domestic ox (see shôr), and according to Mosaic law:

> And every firstling of an ass thou shalt redeem with a lamb . . . (Exodus 13:13).

SYRIAN ONAGER

pere', 'ārôd (?)

Syrian onager or wild ass

Equus hemionus hemippus

The Hebrew and Arabic languages recognize three kinds of asses: one, the chamôr, is clearly the domestic ass or donkey (see chamôr); the others, pere' and 'ārôd, have been translated as wild ass. Several authors have described two distinct species of wild asses from the Holy Land, but there is no evidence to support this. The only species definitely found in the area was the Syrian onager or wild ass, last recorded from the desert north of Aleppo in 1911. The Persian wild ass (*Equus hemionus onager*) still exists but it has not been found in Israel.

The term pere' is most often used; 'ārôd appears only once, in the passage from Job cited below, and in this instance the Revised Standard Version translates it as swift ass. The 'ārôd may have been a domestic ass that became feral.

The Syrian wild ass appears on Assyrian bas-reliefs as a seemingly domesticated animal, yet it is said to be untamable and, even when young, it resists being broken and used as a beast of burden. In a way, it is a symbol of the wilderness:

> Who hath sent out the wild ass [pere'] free? or who hath loosed the bands of the wild ass ['ārôd]?
> Whose house I have made the wilderness, and the barren land his dwellings.
> He scorneth the multitude of the city, neither regardeth he the crying of the driver.
> The range of the mountains is his pasture, and he searcheth after every green thing (Job 39:5-8).

Jeremiah in describing a time of severe drought, refers to the situation of the wild ass:

> The wild asses stand on the bare heights, they pant for air like jackals; their eyes fail because there is no herbage (Jeremiah 14:6; Revised Standard Version).

The Psalmist also mentions the wild ass when water is plentiful:

> They [the springs] give drink to every beast of the field: the wild asses quench their thirst (Psalms 104:11).

chazîr

wild boar, domestic hog

Sus scrofa lybicus

The name chazîr applies to both the wild boar and the domesticated pig. Swine were abhorred by the Phoenicians and were classed as unclean animals under Mosaic law:

> And the swine, though he divide the hoof . . . yet he cheweth not the cud;
> he is unclean to you (Leviticus 11:7).
>
> . . . ye shall not eat of their flesh, nor touch their dead carcase (Deuteronomy 14:8).

The wild boar is widespread in Israel from the coastal plain to the Jordan and Huleh valleys, the mountains of Upper Galilee, and into the desert near the Dead Sea. Apart from the traditional regional prejudice against pigs, it is disliked for its destructiveness to agriculture.

> The boar out of the wood doth waste it . . . (Psalms 80:13).

The wild boar is the largest game animal in Israel. It may eventually become extirpated there as it already has in Egypt.

DOMESTIC HOG

WILD BOAR

re'ēm

aurochs, wild ox, urus, giant ox

Bos primigenius

Re'ēm occurs seven times as the name of a large, powerful, horned animal. The evidence strongly indicates that it was the aurochs, also known as wild ox, giant ox, or urus, an extinct bovine which is believed to be one of the ancestors of domestic cattle.

> . . . they have as it were the horns of the wild ox (Numbers 23:22; Revised Standard Version).

Re'ēm has been translated as unicorn, probably because of a reference to a single horn (Psalms 92:10), but a seal impression from Mesopotamia, c.3000 B.C.E., shows single-horned cattle with the right horn polled. Moreover, the animal's horns are also mentioned in the plural.

In Assyrian records, rīmu was the name of a wild ox with long, strong, thick, curved horns and a hump on its back. It is illustrated in Assyrian sculpture, and the kings of Assyria hunted it in Lebanon and ancient Israel, B.C.E. 884.

> Is the wild ox willing to serve you? Will he spend the night at your crib?
> Can you bind him in the furrow with ropes, or will he harrow the valleys after you?
> Will you depend on him, because his strength is great, and will you leave to him your labor?
> (Job 39:9-11; Revised Standard Version).

DOMESTIC OX

26

(BULL)

AUROCHS

The aurochs existed in southern Syria and northern Israel during the Pleistocene and was found throughout the forests of North Africa, Europe, and southwestern Asia until it became extinct early in the seventeenth century.

shôr, par (bull), pārāh (cow), bāqār (cattle), tsemed (yoke of oxen), 'ēgel (calf)
domestic ox
Bos taurus domesticus

The domestic ox was one of the most important animals in the economy of ancient Israel and was permitted as food (Deuteronomy 14:4-6; 32:14; II Samuel 17:29; Isaiah 7:22).

> So the Lord blessed the latter end of Job more than his beginning;
> for he had . . . a thousand yoke of oxen . . . (Job 42:12).

Oxen were essential for farm work and were often yoked in pairs, but their owners were admonished:

> Thou shalt not plow with an ox and an ass together (Deuteronomy 22:10).

> Thou shalt not muzzle the ox when he treadeth out the corn (Deuteronomy 25:4).

> . . . on the seventh day thou shalt rest: that thine ox and thine ass may rest . . . (Exodus 23:12).

> Thou shalt not see thy brother's ass or his ox fall down by the way, and hide thyself from them:
> thou shalt surely help him to lift them up again (Deuteronomy 22:4).

Oxen were used as beasts of burden:

> . . . brought bread on asses, and on camels, and on mules, and on oxen, and meat, meal,
> cakes of figs, and bunches of raisins, and wine, and oil, and oxen, and sheep abundantly . . .
> (I Chronicles 12:40).

There are references to oxen among animals offered as sacrifices (Numbers 7:3, 17, 21; and Leviticus 17:3-4).

In biblical times, maintaining cattle was difficult because natural fodder was available only in winter and spring.

> And on all hills that shall be digged with the mattock, there shall not come thither the fear
> of briers and thorns: but it shall be for the sending forth of oxen, and for the treading
> of lesser cattle (Isaiah 7:25).

Some cattle were stall-fed:

> Better is a dinner of herbs where love is, then a stalled ox and hatred therewith (Proverbs 15:17).

Several breeds suited to local conditions, such as the small Arab cow, have been developed in the region. Today, with irrigation and improved animal husbandry, the beef and dairy industries in Israel have greatly increased.

'ayyāl

Mesopotamian fallow deer
Dama mesopotamica

'Ayyāl has been translated in the Authorized Version as hart or hind. Although in English usage these terms most often apply to the male and female of the red deer (*Cervus elaphus*), that species has been extinct in southern Syria and northern Palestine since prehistoric times. The particular species of deer intended is the Mesopotamian fallow deer. Fallow deer is used in the Authorized Version as the translation for yachmûr (see yachmûr). The large fallow deer inhabited the forests of Galilee and Mount Carmel and was the symbol of the tribe of Naphtali:

> Naphtali is a hind ['ayyāl; fallow deer] let loose, that bears comely fawns (Genesis 49:21; Revised Standard Version).

Under Mosaic law the fallow deer could be eaten, and it appeared in substantial amounts as daily food at Solomon's table (I Kings 4:23). Its appealing traits were noted in many similes:

(BUCK)

The Lord God is my strength, and he will make my feet like hinds' [fallow deer's] feet, and he will make me to walk upon mine high places (Habbakuk 3:19).

> Then shall the lame men leap as an hart [fallow deer] . . . (Isaiah 35:6).
>
> As the hart [fallow deer] panteth after the water brooks, so panteth my soul after thee, O God (Psalms 42:1).
>
> Let her be as the loving hind [doe] and pleasant roe . . . (Proverbs 5:19).

In the Anchor Bible, this last verse reads:

> A lovable doe! A sweet little mountain goat!

The fallow deer was last seen in Israel in the late nineteenth century and now survives in the wild only in Iran.

(DOE AND FAWN)

MESOPOTAMIAN FALLOW DEER

tsvî

roe deer or gazelle

Gazella capreolus, or *Gazella gazella* and *Gazella dorcas*

The word tsvî was translated as roe in the Authorized Version. In biblical times, as well as at present, laymen probably did not distinguish between the roe deer and the gazelle and most likely called both by the same name. Nor does the Arabic name ghazal differentiate between the two. Both species occurred in the Holy Land, and there are several biblical references to them as an edible animal.

> . . . harts [fallow deer; 'ayyāl], gazelles [or roe; tsvî], roebucks [hartebeest(?); yachmûr], and fatted fowl (I Kings 4:23; Revised Standard Version).

Its swiftness was noted in similes:

> . . . Asahel was as swift of foot as a wild gazelle. (II Samuel 2:18; Revised Standard Version).

> And like a hunted gazelle . . . (Isaiah 13:14; Revised Standard Version).

> . . . save yourself like a gazelle from the hunter . . . (Proverbs 6:5; Revised Standard Version).

ROE DEER   *(DOE)*

(DOE)

ARABIAN GAZELLE

(BUCK)

Apparently both the roe and gazelle were hunted until the twentieth century, when the roe deer finally became extirpated. The gazelles, of which there are two species in Israel, *Gazella gazella* and *Gazella dorcas*, were also threatened with extirpation until the establishment of the State of Israel, when they received total protection. They have recovered in such numbers that in some places they are now pests to agriculture.

29

ARABIAN GAZELLE

DORCAS GAZELLE

ARABIAN ORYX

te'ô

Arabian oryx (*Oryx leucoryx*) (?)

The te'ô is mentioned twice, first among animals that may be eaten, so apparently it was cloven-hoofed and chewed the cud. In the Authorized Version the word has been translated as wild ox or wild bull, but this translation is questionable. Although at least two species of wild ox existed in prehistoric times, the only wild bull that existed in the Holy Land during biblical times was the aurochs (see re'ēm), and that was probably domesticated. The second mention of the te'ô may hold a clue to its identification.

> Thy sons have fainted, they lie at the head of all the streets as a wild bull [te'ô] in a net . . .
> (Isaiah 51:20).

The only wild ungulate that probably inhabited the Holy Land in biblical times and had not already been mentioned in Leviticus is the Arabian oryx. It is a small whitish antelope with long straight horns, which lived in the deserts of the south and east. Great numbers of Arabian oryx have been slaughtered in the past several decades, and it is in danger of extinction. Its identification as an animal of the Bible must remain hypothetical.

ADDAX

BUBAL HARTEBEEST

dîshôn

addax (*Addax nasomaculata*) (?)

The dîshôn is referred to only once, among wild ruminants permitted as food (Deuteronomy 14:5). The reference may be to some species of even-toed ungulate that inhabited the Holy Land at the time (see te'ô). In the Authorized Version it is translated as pygarg (a fictitious animal), following the Greek *pygargos* (literally, white rump) in the Septuagint; the Revised Standard Version translates it as ibex. The addax, an African antelope, was suggested by H. B. Tristram in his *Natural History of the Bible*, but there is no record of the addax's ever having lived anywhere but Africa. It could conceivably have been brought from Egypt where it was hunted, tamed, and kept in captivity. No definitive identification of the dîshôn has yet been made.

yachmûr

bubal hartebeest (*Alcephalus bubalus*) (?)

Yachmûr was translated fallow deer in the Authorized Version and roe buck in the Revised Standard Version. In Arabic the bubal hartebeest is called yachmûr. The hartebeest formerly inhabited Libya and Egypt, where it is now extirpated, and lived in Israel during the Pleistocene period, but there is no record for it outside Africa in historic times.

The yachmûr is mentioned only twice: as permitted for food (Deuteronomy 14:5), and as one of the provisions for Solomon's table (I Kings 4:23). Its identification remains questionable.

gāmāl, bēker, bikrāh
Arabian camel or dromedary
Camelus arabicus

ARABIAN CAMEL

The camel is mentioned many times in the Bible. It was forbidden as food, since its feet bear nails and are not encased in hoofs:

> Nevertheless these shall ye not eat of them that chew the cud, or of them that divideth the hoof;
> as the camel, because he cheweth the cud, but divideth not the hoof; he is unclean unto you
> (Leviticus 11:4; see also Deuteronomy 14:7).

In Israel the camel has been domesticated since biblical times and was used as a beast of burden and as a riding animal:

> And they sat down to eat bread: and they lifted up their eyes and looked, and, behold,
> a company of Ishmaelites came from Gilead with their camels bearing spicery and balm and
> myrrh, going to carry it down to Egypt (Genesis 37:25).

> And she [the Queen of Sheba] came to Jerusalem with a very great train, with camels that bare
> spices, and very much gold, and precious stones . . . (I Kings 10:2).

> And Rebekah lifted up her eyes, and when she saw Isaac, she lighted off the camel (Genesis 24:64).

32

Camels were valuable, and he who owned many was a man of wealth and power:

> And the Midianites and the Amalekites and all the children of the east lay along in the valley like grasshoppers for multitude; and their camels were without number, as the sand by the sea side for multitude (Judges 7:12).

They were counted among the riches of Job, who had three thousand camels before his misfortunes (Job 1:3), and six thousand at the end of his life (Job 42:12), and they are also mentioned as spoils of war:

> And David smote the land, and left neither man nor woman alive, and took away the sheep, and the oxen, and the asses, and camels, and the apparel, and returned, and came to Achish (I Samuel 27:9).
>
> ... The Chaldeans made out three bands, and fell upon the camels, and have carried them away ... (Job 1:17).

The camel was domesticated in Arabia by about 1200 B.C.E., and it no longer exists as a wild animal. Those seen wandering freely in the Negev desert are domesticated and set out to graze, after which they return to their owners of their own free will. Camels are now kept mainly by the Bedouin and are fast disappearing from Israel. The day may yet come when a Bedouin child will have to go to a zoo to see what a camel looks like.

behēmôt
elephant (?), hippopotamus (?), water buffalo (?)

Although the behēmôt (behemoth) is described in great detail, its identification is still unclear. The name is of doubtful derivation. It may be the plural of behēmāh, which in modern Hebrew means beast or cattle. Or it may be the name of a single beast with a plural suffix added to indicate an intensive plural or magnitude. Or it may be the water buffalo, which was known in ancient Mesopotamia. It could possibly be the hippopotamus, which lived in Israel during the Pleistocene and disappeared before historic times but might have been brought back from Egypt where it lived until the nineteenth century. The only reference to the behēmôt is the description which follows:

> Behold now behemoth, which I made with thee; he eateth grass as an ox.
> Lo now, his strength is in his loins, and his force is in the navel of his belly.
> He moveth his tail like a cedar: the sinews of his stones are wrapped together.
> His bones are as strong pieces of brass; his bones are like bars of iron.
> He is the chief of the ways of God: he that made him can make his sword to approach unto him.
> Surely the mountains bring him forth food, where all the beasts of the field play.
> He lieth under the shady trees, in the covert of the reed, and fens.

ELEPHANT

The shady trees cover him with their shadow; the willows of the brook compass him about.
Behold, he drinketh up a river, and hasteth not: he trusteth that he can draw up Jordan
into his mouth.
He taketh it with his eyes: his nose pierceth through snares (Job 40:15-24).

In many ways this passage suggests the elephant more than the hippopotamus. The
comparison of the animal's tail to a cedar is quite appropriate for the elephant, whose tail has a brush-
like tuft of stiff hairs and can reach a length of about 52 inches. The importation of elephants' tusks
is mentioned in I Kings 10:22. In prehistoric times, the elephant did live in the Holy Land. A race of
the Indian elephant was found in Syria as recently as 859–833 B.C.E. During the third century B.C.E.,
elephants of a small race were captured in Ethiopia, trained by the Ptolemies, and brought to Egypt
for use in warfare. In the Book of the Maccabees it is told that elephants were employed in the army
of Antiochus Epiphanes against the Jews.

DOMESTIC SHEEP

keves, 'ayil (ram), **kivsāh** (ewe), **kārîm** (lambs), **tsō'n** (flock of sheep and goats) domestic sheep
Ovis aries

Domestic sheep have been important in the life and economy of the Holy Land since biblical times. First mentioned in connection with Cain and Abel (Genesis 4:2), sheep, both adults and lambs, were offered for sacrifice (Genesis 15:9; Exodus 20:24, 29:38, Leviticus 9:3, 12:6), or as a tribute (II Kings 3:4). In the story of the sacrifice of Isaac, a ram is offered in place of Abraham's son:

> And Abraham lifted up his eyes and looked, and behold, behind him was a ram, caught in a thicket by his horns . . . (Genesis 22:13).

Domestic sheep were eaten (I Samuel 25:18), used for clothing (Leviticus 13:47), and as a covering for the tabernacle (Exodus 25:5). Domestic sheep may have been bred from some living species of wild sheep, as no remains of any wild *Ovis aries* have been discovered, although fossil bones have been found in sites of human settlement which date back to 5000 B.C.E. No one knows what the domestic sheep of biblical times looked like. The most popular strain of sheep in Israel today is the fat-tailed sheep (*Ovis aries platura;* awassi in Arabic). It originated in Spain and was brought to Palestine from Germany.

zemer

ruminating ungulate, mouflon (*Ovis musimon*) (?)

The zemer is listed among edible ruminating ungulates in Deuteronomy 14:5. In the Authorized Version it was translated as chamois and some have considered it to be the giraffe, but neither of these species lived in the Holy Land. Two other possible identifications are the aoudad or Barbary sheep, which lived on the Egyptian side of the Red Sea although there is no reliable data for it from the Holy Land, and another wild sheep called the mouflon which is found in Cyprus. In view of the proximity of that island, where settled life goes back to at least 5000 B.C.E., it is plausible that the domesticated mouflon could have been brought from there. But whether any of these species has claim to the name zemer is sheer speculation.

CYPRIAN MOUFLON

yā‘ēl, ’aqqô (?)
wild goat, Nubian ibex
Capra ibex nubiana

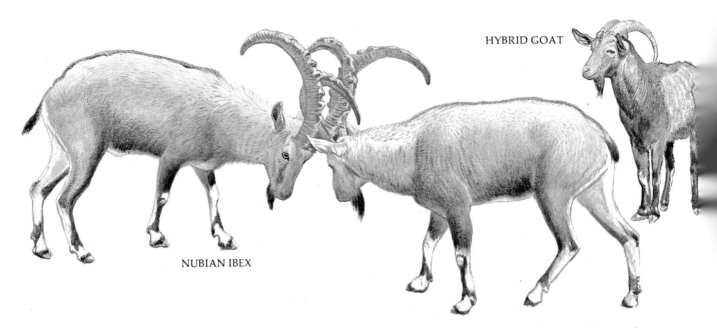

HYBRID GOAT

NUBIAN IBEX

There are several references to the yā‘ēl, which is translated as wild goat. According to Mosaic dietary laws, it may be eaten. Its habitat is mentioned:

> The high hills are a refuge for the wild goats . . . (Psalms 104:18).

and a refuge for David as well:

> Then Saul . . . went to seek David and his men upon the rocks of the wild goats (I Samuel 24:2).

There is a reference to its foaling:

> Knowest thou the time when the wild goats of the rocks bring forth? . . .
> Canst thou number the months that they fulfill? . . . (Job 39:1,2).

On the shore of the Dead Sea is an oasis named Ein Gedi, meaning Spring of the Kid. This region is frequented today by a population of Nubian ibex, much as it must have been in biblical times. It seems reasonable to identify the wild goat of the Bible with the Nubian ibex. One of the most impressive of native wild animals, the ibex was threatened by extinction less than three decades ago. With complete protection, it has made a welcome comeback.

Another suggested identification for the wild goat of the Scriptures is the bezoar (*Capra aegagrus*). Fossil remains indicate that this species may have ranged as far south as northern Israel in prehistoric times. (See illustration on page 9.)

The name ’aqqô appears only once—among edible mammals (Deuteronomy 14:5); it has been translated as wild goat, but the identification is questionable.

36

DOMESTIC GOAT

tayish, tsāfîr, śā'îr (male), **'ēz** (female), **gedî** (kid)
domestic goat
Capra hircus

One of the most important animals in the economy of the pastoral peoples of the Bible was the goat. Its remains have been traced back to about 8500 B.C.E. at Jericho, and it may have been the earliest ruminant to have been domesticated. This ancient domestic goat was probably a type of bezoar, or true goat, and not an ibex. In biblical times, goatskin was made into garments and water bottles and goat hair was woven into fabrics (Exodus 26:7). It was a staple source of food:

> These are the beasts which ye shall eat: the ox, the sheep and the goat (Deuteronomy 14:4).

> And thou shalt have goat's milk enough for thy food, for the food of thy household, and for the maintenance for thy maidens (Proverbs 27:27).

One of the principal origins of Jewish dietary laws appears very early:

> Thou shalt not seethe a kid in his mother's milk. (Deuteronomy 14:21).

The goat is frequently mentioned as a sacrificial offering:

> And if his offering be a goat, then he shall offer it before the Lord (Leviticus 3:12).

> Or if his sin, wherein he hath sinned, come to his knowledge; he shalt bring his offering, a kid of the goats, a male without blemish (Leviticus 4:23).

Breeds of goat now occurring in Israel are the floppy-eared mamber goat, a long-haired breed which probably originated in eastern Asia, and the white angora goat. Domestic goats have been largely to blame for the degraded condition of the forests of the Middle East, since their constant browsing prevents trees from reaching maximum growth.

The śā'îr appears many times in the Bible. The Hebrew word signifies hairy or shaggy; in modern Hebrew it means he-goat. In enumerating procedures of sacrifices it is translated as goat (Numbers 7:16,22). It also appears as the scapegoat (Leviticus 16:10). Several times the word occurs in connections where the context precludes the possibility of reference to a goat; for example, II Chronicles 11:15, where it is translated in the Authorized Version as devil and in the Anchor Bible as satyr.

> The satyr [śā'îr] shall cry to his fellow (Isaiah 34:14).

In speaking of the desolation of Babylon Isaiah says:

> But wild beasts of the desert shall lie there ... and satyrs [śā'îrim] shall dance there (Isaiah 13:21).

'arnevet
Cape hare
Lepus capensis

The 'arnevet or hare was among the animals forbidden as food by Mosaic law (Deuteronomy 14:7). It was erroneously thought to be a ruminant because of the way it moves its jaw while eating.

> And the hare, because he cheweth the cud, but divideth not the hoof; he is unclean unto you (Leviticus 11:6).

In English translations of the Septuagint, this animal is mistakenly given as hedgehog. Cape hares are common and widespread throughout Israel. There are at least two distinct populations: a shorter-eared northern race and a longer-eared desert race south of Beersheba.

SYRIAN HARE

chōled, chafarfērôth
mole-rat
Spalax leucodon

MOLE-RAT

Chōled, an unclean animal (Leviticus 11:29), has been translated as weasel and as polecat. The root of chōled means "to dig," the name may be allied to the Arabic khuld, which means mole-rat. Although the marbled polecat (*Vormela peregusna*) is found in Israel, and weasels are known from Lebanon (there have been unconfirmed reports from Mount Tabor), neither is noted for digging. Mole-rat is now the accepted translation. Chafarfērôth is translated as mole (Isaiah 2:20), but since there are no moles in Israel, this term may also refer to the mole-rat. The root of chafar means "to burrow," and the mole-rat builds an underground tunnel marked by a series of upturned mounds of earth. It is a sausage-shaped rat, with silky, silvery fur, and without eyes, external ears, or tail. It lives underground and feeds on plants and is a pest in gardens and to agriculture in Israel, where it is common and widely distributed.

'akbār

mouse, rat, gerbil, jird, jerboa, hamster, social vole
Muridae, Dipodidae

The 'akbār is mentioned several times, twice as an unclean animal (Leviticus 11:29 and Isaiah 66:17). The reference could be to the hamster, which is eaten in northern Syria, but probably 'akbār is a generic name, denoting the house mouse and rat and also including other small rodents, of which there are twenty-two species in Israel. In one case it may refer to a particular species, the social vole (*Microtus socialus*). When the Philistines detained the Ark of the Covenant, a plague of mice was inflicted upon them:

> . . . your mice that mar the land . . . (I Samuel 6:5).

This almost certainly refers to the social vole, which is commonly found throughout the Mediterranean region of Israel, including the land of the Philistines. The biblical plague is comparable to the periodic outbreaks of voles which still occur and are highly destructive to agriculture.

HOUSE MOUSE

SOCIAL VOLE

tachash

porpoise, dolphin (*Tursiops aduncus*) (?); dugong (*Halicore dugong hemprichii*) (?)

Skins of the tachash are among the offerings listed in the preparation of the Sanctuary (Exodus 25:5). In nearly all the ancient versions, the word tachash designates a color, either black or blue, and not an animal. In the Authorized Version it was translated as badger, but this is now generally conceded to be incorrect. The skins referred to are more probably those of some marine animal. In Arabic, tukhas means dolphin, seal, or whale, and these animals, except the seal, do occur in the Red Sea, though they are rarely seen along the coast. The similarly shaped dugong, which inhabits the coastal water and estuaries of the Red Sea and is sometimes caught in fisherman's nets, is another possibility. It may have been common in biblical days, but because it was highly prized not only for its flesh and oil but for reputed aphrodisiac properties, its numbers are now greatly decreased.

Tachash skins are mentioned as an outer covering for the Tabernacle (Exodus 26:14), and as shoes:

> I clothed you also with embroidered cloth and shod you with leather [tachash] . . .
> (Ezekiel 16:10; Revised Standard Version).

SPERM WHALE

BOTTLE-NOSED DOLPHIN

DUGONG

tannîn (*pl.*, tannînim)
whale, dolphin (Cetaceadae) (?); sea monster

In the Authorized Version tannîn is translated variously as whale, sea monster, serpent, and dragon. In modern Hebrew the word means crocodile (see livyātān).

The tannîn is usually mentioned in connection with the sea; the word may be a generic term for large animals that move in the deep waters.

> So God created the great sea monsters [tannînim] and every living creature that moves, with which the waters swarm, according to their kinds . . . (Genesis 1:21; Revised Standard Version).

> Praise the Lord from the earth, ye dragons [tannînim], and all deeps. (Psalms 148:7).

> Am I the sea, or a sea monster [tannîn] that thou settest a guard over me? (Job 7:12; Revised Standard Version).

In the story of Aaron's rod, the translation is serpent:

> . . . Take thy rod, and cast it before Pharaoh, and it shall become a serpent [tannîn] . . .

> For they cast down every man his rod, and they became serpents [tannînim]; but Aaron's rod swallowed up their rods (Exodus 7:9, 12).

Its identification as a mammal is based on the following passage:

> Even the sea monsters [tannînim] draw out the breast, they give suck to their young ones . . . (Lamentations 4:3).

However, the Anchor Bible points out that jackals [tannîm] must have been intended here (see tan) and so translates the word.

Several species of whales occur in the Mediterranean, although they are rare. Even if they were more numerous in biblical times, they would probably have been little known, since the Israelites were not a maritime people. Two species of dolphin, which reach a length of up to 12 feet, are also found in the Mediterranean and occasionally one is washed ashore. In a reference to the story of Jonah in Matthew 12:40 the Hebrew word dag, meaning fish, was given in Greek as *kētos* and translated as whale (see dag).

REED WARBLER

BIRDS

tsippôr (*pl.*, tsippôrîm), 'ôf
bird, fowl
Aves

The word tsippôr occurs many times in the Bible and is usually translated as bird.

Most birds were not specified but were called tsippôrîm collectively. References were made to their nest or song:

> As a bird that wandereth from her nest, so is a man that wandereth from his place (Proverbs 27:8).

> . . . the time of the singing of birds is come . . . (Song of Solomon 2:12).

Perhaps the first instance of conservation or protection of birds dates back to biblical times:

> If a bird's nest chance to be before thee in the way in any tree, or on the ground, whether they be young ones, or eggs, and the dam sitting upon the young, or upon the eggs, thou shalt not take the dam with the young;
> But thou shalt in any wise let the dam go, and take the young to thee; that it may be well with thee, and that thou mayest prolong thy days (Deuteronomy 22:6-7).

The word 'ôf has been translated as fowl, but the references indicate that the term was used for any winged or flying animal—bird, beetle, or bat—or for all such animals, as in the story of Creation (Genesis 2:19).

> By them [the springs in the valleys] shall the fowls of the heaven have their habitation, which sing among the branches (Psalms 104:12).

> All fowls that creep, going upon all fours, shall be an abomination unto you (Leviticus 11:20).

42

qā'at
desert bird (?), owl (?)

The qā'at is mentioned several times and is listed among the unclean
birds (Leviticus 11:18; Deuteronomy 14:17), where it was translated as
pelican. The Hebrew word qē' means vomit, and this possibly suggests the
manner in which the qā'at feeds its young. The juvenile of the pelican places
its bill inside the throat of the parent, which then regurgitates half-digested
fish. However, the pelican is only a passing migrant in Israel; it does not
breed there, nor is there any evidence that it ever did. The pygmy cormorant,
which feeds its young in a similar way, formerly bred in Israel. A number of
other birds, including herons and gulls, also disgorge food when feeding their
young, and owls throw up pellets. The name qā'at could be generic, applying
to any of these, but for the fact that it is described as inhabiting deserts
and waste places (Isaiah 34:11,15).

> I am like an owl [qā'at] of the desert (Psalms 102:6).

The jackdaw (*Corvus monedula*) has been suggested, but it is not
a bird of the desert. Such a habitat is suitable only for the owl among the
birds mentioned. The identity of the qā'at remains unknown.

qippōd
passerine bird (?)

The qippōd occurs three times in the Old Testament: Isaiah 14:23 and
34:11 and Zephaniah 2:14. In all cases it is depicted as inhabiting desolate
ruins, along with owls, ravens, and other birds or animals. In the Authorized
Version it is translated as bittern; in the Revised Standard Version and
elsewhere the translation, following the Septuagint and the Vulgate, is
porcupine or hedgehog. The Anchor Bible points out that ruins were
generally believed to be occupied not only by birds, snakes, and other
animals but also by spirits and demons; the word qippōd, therefore, may
refer to something supernatural. In modern Hebrew it means hedgehog.

'anāfāh

heron or egret (Ardeidae) (?)

The 'anāfāh appears only in the listing of unclean birds (Leviticus 11:19; Deuteronomy 14:18). There it is translated as heron, which is also the meaning in modern Hebrew. If the translation is correct, it would indicate a generic name, as there are seven common species of herons and egrets and two species of bitterns.

PURPLE HERON

Israel and Sinai lie in the direct line of migration for storks between eastern Europe and Africa. The punctual appearance of great numbers of migrating storks every spring was noted in biblical times:

> Even the stork in the heaven knows her times . . .
> (Jeremiah 8:7; Revised Standard Version).

> Then I lifted up mine eyes, and looked, and, behold, there came out two women, and the wind was in their wings; for they had wings like the wings of a stork . . .
> (Zechariah 5:9).

> . . . as for the stork, the fir trees are her house
> (Psalms 104:17).

"Fir trees" may refer more specifically to the cedars of Lebanon. Although the stork is still generally common, it has grown rare as a breeding bird in many of its old haunts in Europe. Recently it was found breeding in Israel, after an absence possibly since biblical times.

chasîdāḥ

white stork

Ciconia ciconia

WHITE STORK

SYRIAN OSTRICH

yā'ēn, bat ya'anāh

Syrian ostrich

Struthio camelus syriacus

With one exception, the name for ostrich is in the feminine
form. It has sometimes been translated as owl or peacock and
is listed among unclean birds (Leviticus 11:16; Deuteronomy 14:15).

> I am a brother of jackals, and a companion of ostriches
> (Job 30:29; Revised Standard Version).

> . . . I will go stripped and naked; I will make lamentation
> like the jackals, and mourning like the ostriches (Micah 1:8;
> Revised Standard Version).

The word mourning does not exactly suggest the voice of an
ostrich, which is a loud hiss and booming roar.

In lamenting the sins of Zion, Jeremiah said:

> . . . the daughter of my people has become cruel,
> like the ostriches in the wilderness (Lamentations 4:3;
> Revised Standard Version).

Describing the fall of Babylon, Isaiah prophesied:

> But wild beasts of the desert will lie down there, and its houses will be full of howling creatures; there ostriches will dwell . . . (Isaiah 13:21; Revised Standard Version).

> . . . It shall be the haunt of jackals, an abode for ostriches (Isaiah 34:13; Revised Standard Version).

The following passage gives a detailed account of habits that were ascribed (sometimes mistakenly) to the ostrich. In the Hebrew the word chasîdāh (stork) seems to be included, but this is obviously an error in transcription. The English versions correctly translate it as ostrich.

> Gavest thou . . . wings and feathers unto the ostrich?
> Which leaveth her eggs in the earth, and warmeth them in dust.
> And forgetteth that the foot may crush them, or that the wild beast may break them.
> She is hardened against her young ones, as though they were not hers: her labour is in vain without fear;
> Because God hath deprived her of wisdom, neither hath he imparted to her understanding.
> What time she lifted up herself on high, she scorneth the horse and his rider (Job 39:13-18).

The ostrich is the largest living bird, standing 8 feet tall and weighing over 300 pounds. Its eggs are laid on the ground. It is the swiftest of all cursorial birds, and running ostriches have been clocked at 30 miles per hour. The Syrian ostrich formerly inhabited the deserts of Israel and Sinai, but the last specimen was reported killed and eaten by Arabs in Saudi Arabia during World War II and the bird is now considered extinct.

shālāk
plunging bird (?)

The word shālāk appears only in reference to an unclean
bird (Leviticus 11:17; Deuteronomy 14:17), where it is translated
as cormorant. The etymology suggests some sort of plunging bird,
but there are a number of species more conspicuous for this habit
than the cormorant, which simply dives from the surface of the
water. Kingfishers (Alcedinidae) and terns (Sternidae) are more
common and very noticeable for their plunging from high in
the air into water. The osprey (*Paridion haliaërus*), which
plunges feet first, is called shālāk in modern Hebrew. It is
possible that shālāk was generic for plunging birds.

barburîm 'abusîm
fatted fowl, domestic goose, domestic fowl
Anser anser domesticus, Gallus gallus domesticus

Barburîm 'abusîm, translated as fatted fowl, is mentioned among
Solomon's provisions (I Kings 4:23). Fatted fowl is thought to
refer to geese, as no other domestic bird except for the pigeon
is mentioned. Barnyard geese are descended from the grey
lag goose of northern Europe and were probably among the
first birds to be domesticated by man. Domestic fowl were
imported from Asia, where they are believed to have originated
from the jungle fowl. After the Babylonian captivity they were
found in the Holy Land. A seal bearing the name of Jaazaniah
(see II Kings 25:23) shows a fighting cock, indicating that
these birds were known from Israel as early as 587 B.C.E.

There are several references to domesticated fowl in
the New Testament (Matthew 23:37; 26:34,75; Mark 14:30,72;
Luke 22:34), but whether the Greek term used there represents
this Hebrew expression is not clear.

DOMESTIC GOOSE

GREYLAG GOOSE

(HEN)

(COCK)

JUNGLE FOWL

(COCK)

DOMESTIC FOWL

EGYPTIAN VULTURE

nesher, ayyāh, dāyāh (*pl.,* **dayôt**), **rāchām**
vulture, eagle, kite
Falconidae, Accipitridae

Several different words have been translated as vulture, eagle, or kite. They are all grouped as unclean birds (Leviticus 11:13, 14, 18; Deuteronomy 14:12, 13). Again it is likely that the ancient Hebrews, like laymen of today, did not distinguish between similar species, and the word nesher, which appears most often, probably applied to both the vulture and the eagle. Certainly, when the attribute of flight is mentioned, either is possible; however, the translation is usually eagle.

> There be three things which are too wonderful for me, yea, four of which I know not:
> The way of an eagle in the air . . . (Proverbs 30:18-19).
>
> . . . they shall mount up with wings as eagles . . . (Isaiah 40:31).
>
> Ye have seen what I did unto the Egyptians, and how I bare you on eagles' wings, and brought you unto myself (Exodus 19:4).
>
> Our persecutors are swifter than the eagles of the heavens: they pursued us upon the mountains, they laid wait for us in the wilderness (Lamentations 4:19).
>
> . . . his horses are swifter than eagles (Jeremiah 4:13).
>
> . . . they shall fly as the eagle that hasteth to eat (Habakkuk 1:8).

The following passage clearly describes the vulture:

> Make thee bald, and poll thee for thy delicate children: enlarge thy baldness as the eagle [vulture] . . . (Micah 1:16).

The ayyāh may be another keen-sighted scavenger such as the common black kite (Job 28:7). The dāyāh is mentioned by Isaiah in describing a scene of desolation:

> . . . there shall the vultures [dayôt] also be gathered, every one with her mate (Isaiah 34:15).

The identification as vulture is questionable.

The rāchām, translated as gier-eagle in the Authorized Version and as carrion vulture in the Revised Standard Version appears only once, among the unclean birds (Leviticus 11:18). Again, the identification is doubtful.

BLACK KITE

(ADULT)

LESSER SPOTTED EAGLE

(IMMATURE)

51

peres
lammergeier or bearded vulture
Gypaetus barbatus

LAMMERGEIER

The word peres occurs only among birds that are an abomination (Leviticus 11:13; Deuteronomy 14:12). It is translated in the Authorized Version as ossifrage, which by derivation means bone-breaker. In Hebrew peres means smasher, suggesting the habit of the lammergeier, which drops its prey from great heights. The lammergeier is one of the largest birds of prey. It has become increasingly scarce in the mountains of Europe and Asia but still survives in Israel and Sinai.

GRIFFON

LONG-LEGGED BUZZARD

nēts

hawk, falcon

Falconidae

The word nēts is translated as hawk and appears to be a generic term applied to all keen-sighted birds of prey with the exception of vultures and eagles. It is listed among birds of abomination which were not to be eaten (Deuteronomy 14:15). The annual migration of hawks and other raptors through Israel, particularly in the desert region, is a most spectacular sight. Tens of thousands of eagles, hawks, kites, harriers, falcons of all kinds can be observed today, much as they must have been noticed in biblical times.

> Doth the hawk soar by thy wisdom, and stretch her wings toward the south? (Job 39:26).

'oznîyyāh

bird of prey (?)

The 'oznîyyāh appears only among the listing of unclean birds of prey (Leviticus 11:13; Deuteronomy 14:12), where it is translated in the Authorized Version as osprey (*Pandion haliaetus*). Other speculations include the short-toed eagle (*Circaetus gallicus*) and white-tailed sea eagle (*Haliaetus albicella*). The root of 'oznîyyāh is not known; it may be a foreign word used in Hebrew.

LITTLE OWL

WHITE OWL

EAGLE OWL

kôs, yanshûf, qippôz, tinshemet, lîlît

little owl, great owl, white owl (?), night bird (?)

Strigidae

Several kinds of unclean birds have been translated as owls in Deuteronomy 14:16 in the Authorized Version. If owls were indeed intended, it is surprising and inconsistent that they were mentioned specifically, instead of generically, as are other similar groups.

Two words, yanshûf and qippôz, have been translated as eagle owl or great owl. This is the largest species of owl found in Israel and is a resident throughout the country.

> There shall the great owl [qippôz] make her nest, and lay,
> and hatch, and gather under her shadow . . . (Isaiah 34:15).

In the Moffat translation, qippôz is given as arrow snake. The Anchor Bible uses snake but mentions the possibility that an imaginary animal or a spirit may be intended (see qippōd).

The kôs, or little owl, is common throughout the country. Partly diurnal in habit, it is the most conspicuous of owls.

In modern Hebrew tinshemet means barn owl or white owl. The tinshemet appears twice in the lists of restricted foods—once among owls where it has been translated as swan, and once among creeping things where it has been translated as mole. It probably does not refer to the swan, since duck and goose, which belong to the same family, may be eaten. In Israel today the swan is very rare.

The Hebrew name lîlît means "something of the night"; the Authorized Version translates it as screech owl. In discussing the indignation of the Lord with all nations, and the devastation that would occur, Isaiah says:

> . . . the screech owl [lîlît] also shall rest there and find
> for herself a place of rest (Isaiah 34:14).

In the Revised Standard Version and the Anchor Bible, lîlît is here translated as night hag. In legend the lîlît is a spirit in the form of a beautiful woman that lures men. The author, on hearing for the first time a sweet, clear call in the middle of the night, followed the sound through the dark streets and found a little scops owl sitting in a tall tree. In biblical times, only a reckless fool would have followed such a call.

qōrē

sand partridge, chukar

Ammoperdix heyi, Alectoris chukar

Two species of partridge are found in Israel, the sand partridge, confined to the desert, and the chukar, common throughout the country. The ancient Hebrews do not seem to have distinguished between the two, calling them both qōrē, which is translated as partridge. Partridges were favorite game birds in biblical times just as they are today. David said of his persecution by Saul:

> . . . as when one doth hunt a partridge in the mountains
> (I Samuel 26:20).

Jeremiah, referring to the unrighteous acquirement of riches, uses the comparison:

> As the partridge sitteth on eggs, and hatcheth them
> not . . . (Jeremiah 17:11).

HEY'S SAND PARTRIDGE

CHUKAR

QUAIL

slāv

quail

Coturnix coturnix

There seems to be no reason to doubt that the word slāv in the Pentateuch denotes the common quail.

> And it came to pass, that at even the quails came up,
> and covered the camp (Exodus 16:13).

> And there went forth a wind from the Lord, and brought
> quails from the sea, and let them fall by the camp,
> as it were a day's journey on this side, and as it were
> a day's journey on the other side, round about the camp,
> and as it were two cubits high upon the face of the earth
> (Numbers 11:31).

This incident is also mentioned in Psalms:

> The people asked, and he brought quails, and satisfied
> them with the bread of heaven (Psalms 105:40).

The numbers of quail that migrate across the Mediterranean were reported by Pliny the Elder in his *Natural History* as so enormous that they sometimes sank the vessels on which they had alighted. On the island of Capri, 160,000 quail were stated to have been netted in one season. At the time of the event narrated in Scripture, the quail were on their migration northward and must have arrived from the other side of the Gulf of Suez. Migrating quail are said to land from their flight across the sea so exhausted that besides being taken in nets they are easily picked up from the ground by hand. The quail is a common passing migrant and summer visitor in Israel. It is still caught in nets by the Bedouin of Sinai.

COMMON PEAFOWL

tukkî (*pl.*, **tukkîyyîm**)

common peafowl or peacock (*Pavo cristatus*) (?), monkey (?)

Tukkîyyîm, mentioned among the products brought home to Jerusalem by King Solomon's navy of Tarshish (I Kings 10:22; II Chronicles 9:21), has traditionally been translated as peacocks. The Hebrew word may be related to the Tamil tokei, meaning peacock; a similar word is still used in Ceylon, where peafowl are native, and the King's navy may have visited southern India or Ceylon to bring back the gold and ivory which are also mentioned. However, some prefer a derivation from an Egyptian word referring to a type of monkey (see qôf). The translation is open to question.

tachmās

an unclean bird

NUBIAN NIGHTJAR

The word tachmās appears in the lists of birds forbidden as food by Mosaic law (Leviticus 11:16; Deuteronomy 14:15). The name may come from the root CH-M-S, meaning "to take forcibly," which would suggest a predatory bird. However, in the Authorized Version it was translated as nighthawk (nightjar, *Caprimulgus* species), a bird which is not predatory. Three species of nightjar occur in Israel, but the identification of the tachmās is open to question.

yônāh (adult), **gôzāl** (squab)
rock dove or pigeon
Columba livia

Pigeons and doves are mentioned in the Bible more often than any other birds. One of the first birds referred to is the dove sent forth from the Ark by Noah (Genesis 8:8-12). Its return with an olive branch in its mouth has become a symbol of peace. Pigeons were popular offerings for various occasions:

> And he said unto him, Take me . . . a turtledove, and a young pigeon (Genesis 15:9).

> On the eighth day he shall bring two turtledoves or two young pigeons to the priest . . . (Numbers 6:10; Revised Standard Version).

The dove is often used as a simile:

> . . . I did mourn as a dove . . . (Isaiah 38:14).

> . . . the wings of the dove plated with silver, and her pinions with yellow gold (Psalms 68:14; Anchor Bible).

> But they that escape of them shall escape, and shall be on the mountains like doves of the valleys, all of them mourning, every one for his iniquity (Ezekiel 7:16).

> His eyes are as the eyes of doves . . . (Song of Solomon 5:12).

> And I said, Oh that I had wings like a dove! for then would I fly away, and be at rest (Psalms 55:6).

In condemning Moab, the prophet Jeremiah said:

> O ye that dwell in Moab, leave the cities, and dwell in the rock, and be like the dove that maketh her nest in the sides of the hole's mouth (Jeremiah 48:28).

The rock dove, *Columba livia*, is the wild ancestor of the city pigeon and lives on rocky mountains throughout the country. Domesticated breeds are kept today.

ROCK DOVE

tôr

turtledove

Streptopelia species

TURTLEDOVE

The name tôr may be onomatopoeic, derived from the plaintive cooing of the turtledove. Its voice was the symbol of spring:

> For lo, the winter is past, the rain is over and gone.
> The flowers appear on the earth; the time of singing has come,
> and the voice of the turtledove is heard in the land
> (Song of Solomon 2:11-12; Revised Standard Version).

The Psalmist in his lament to God compared himself to the turtledove:

> O deliver not the soul of thy turtledove unto the multitude of the wicked . . . (Psalms 74:19).

Turtledoves as well as rock doves were commonly offered for sacrifice in biblical times:

> And if the burnt sacrifice for his offering to the Lord be of fowls, then he shall bring his offering of turtledoves or of young pigeons. (Leviticus 1:14).

It has been suggested that the substitution of turtledoves or young pigeons for a lamb or kid was a concession to the poor.

Besides the turtledove (*Streptopelia turtur*), which migrates through Israel in great numbers and also remains to breed, the collared turtledove (*S. decaecto*) and the palm dove (*S. senegalensis*) are common permanent residents.

BROWN-NECKED RAVEN

'ōrēv

crow or raven

Corvus species

Apparently the word 'ōrēv is generic for the whole tribe of crows, ravens, rooks, jackdaws, and jays, all of which occur in Israel. It has generally been translated as raven and appears time and again in the Bible.

> And the ravens brought him [Elijah] bread and flesh in the morning, and bread and flesh in the evening; and he drank of the brook (I Kings 17:6).
>
> . . . his locks are . . . black as a raven (Song of Solomon 5:11).
>
> He giveth to the beast his food, and to the young ravens which cry (Psalms 147:9).
>
> The eye that mocketh at his father, and despiseth to obey his mother, the ravens of the valley shall pick it out . . . (Proverbs 30:17).

In the story of Noah, the raven was the first bird to be released from the ark:

> And he sent forth a raven, which went forth to and fro until the waters were dried up from off the earth (Genesis 8:7).

Three species of ravans occur in Israel. The European raven (*Corvus corax*) inhabits the northern mountains. The brown-necked raven (*C. ruficollis*) is common throughout the desert up to the Judean hills and around Jerusalem. The fan-tailed raven (*C. rhipidurus*) is confined to the Dead Sea region and the Arava.

The raven is mentioned as a bird of abomination, which may not be eaten:

> Every raven after his kind (Leviticus 11:15).

shachaf

an unclean bird

The shachaf appears only in the lists of unclean birds (Leviticus 11:16; Deuteronomy 14:15) where it is translated as cuckoo in the Authorized Version, as sea mew in the American Revised Version, and as sea gull in the Revised Standard Version. In modern Hebrew the word means gull; it may come from the same root as shachefet, the modern Hebrew word for tuberculosis.

Two species of cuckoos occur in Israel: the European cuckoo (*Cuculus canorus*) and the great spotted cuckoo (*Clemator glandarius*). Both are inconspicuous passing migrants, although the latter remains to breed. The term shachaf could be generic for the gull family, regarded as unclean because of their scavenging habits. The identification remains questionable.

HERRING GULL

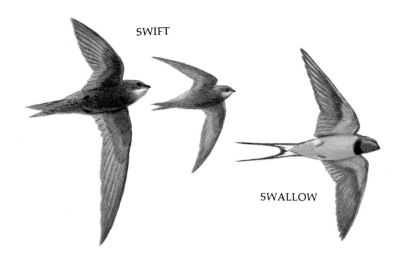

SWIFT

SWALLOW

sîs, ʿāgûr

swift (?), swallow (?)

Sîs and ʿāgûr are obviously migratory birds whose arrival is conspicuous. The Authorized Version has:

> . . . and the crane [sîs] and the swallow [ʿāgûr] observe the time of their coming . . . (Jeremiah 8:7).

> . . . like a crane [sîs] or a swallow [ʿāgûr] so did I chatter . . . (Isaiah 38:14).

The Revised Standard Version reads swallow and crane, and the Anchor Bible swift and thrush.

Both passages aptly describe the swifts, which arrive quite suddenly and conspicuously in the cities during March and swoop and screech above the streets in great numbers, departing equally suddenly in June. Swallows have a twittering call and are mostly migratory, at times passing through the countryside in large numbers. Although of different families, the swallow and the swift are similar in appearance and may have been called by the same name.

Cranes are relatively inconspicuous in arrival and frequent remote areas. The thrush seems unlikely; with the exception of the field fare, no thrushes arrive in flocks and none are noisy. The starling or the wagtail or some other prominent migratory bird may be intended.

drôr

house sparrow (*Passer domesticus biblicus*) (?)

Drôr has been translated as swallow, but so have other words (see ʿāgûr, sîs). Tsippôr, which seems to be generic for birds (see tsippôr), is twice translated as sparrow in the Authorized Version.

> Yea, the sparrow [tsippôr] hath found a house, and the swallow [drôr] a nest for herself, where she may lay her young, even thine altars, O Lord of Hosts . . . (Psalms 84:3).

In the following passage the reference to a solitary bird does not fit the gregarious nature of the house sparrow, and the Revised Standard Version gives "lonely bird" instead.

> I watch, and am as a sparrow [tsippôr] alone upon the house top (Psalms 102:7).

Both swallows and sparrows nest in and around houses.
The swallow *Hirunda rustica* constructs its nest on rafters and the
red-rumped swallow *H. daurica* builds an enclosed mud nest on a wall.
The sparrow stuffs its untidy nest into any space available. The drôr
seems most likely to be the ubiquitous house sparrow, found
throughout Israel wherever there is human habitation.

(FEMALE) (MALE)

HOOPOE

HOUSE SPARROW

dûkîfat
hoopoe
Upupa epops

The dûkîfat occurs only in Leviticus 11:19 and the parallel passage in
Deuteronomy 14:18, where it appears among the birds forbidden as
food. It is translated in the Authorized Version as lapwing, but
commentators generally agree that the hoopoe was intended instead.
The hoopoe has a rancid odor and is generally left alone
by cats and other predators.

According to legend, the hoopoe carried letters between
Solomon and the Queen of Sheba. It is common throughout Israel
today and often nests in holes in and around human habitations.

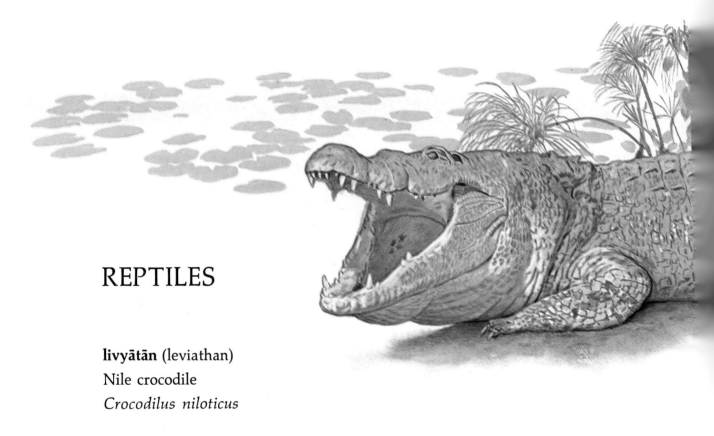

REPTILES

livyātān (leviathan)
Nile crocodile
Crocodilus niloticus

Livyātān (leviathan) appears several times to denote a kind of
aquatic animal. In modern Hebrew it means whale, but some of
the most descriptive passages about the livyātān in the Bible appear
to apply to the crocodile; for example:

> Who can open the doors of his face? his teeth are terrible
> round about.
> His scales are his pride, shut up together as with a close seal.
> One is so near to another, that no air can come between
> them . . .
> Sharp stones are under him: he spreadeth sharp pointed
> things upon the mire (Job 41:14–16, 30).

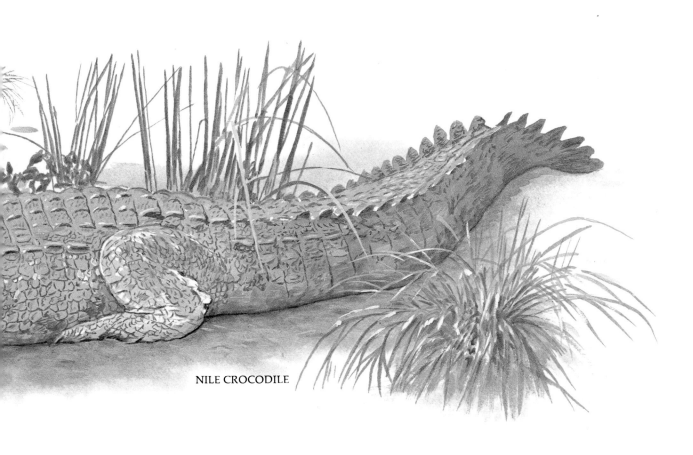

NILE CROCODILE

In another passage the word tannîm (see tan, tannîn) quite clearly refers to the crocodile, although it is translated as dragon:

> . . . Behold, I am against thee, Pharaoh, king of Egypt, the great dragon [tannîm] that lieth in the midst of his rivers . . . (Ezekiel 29:3).

The crocodile inhabited the lower Nile before it was extirpated there. It may have arrived on the coast of Israel (the only place the crocodile occurred outside of Africa) via the Mediterranean. It lived in the river Zurka (Nachal Tananim) which flows through the coastal plain, but the last capture of one occurred in the nineteenth century.

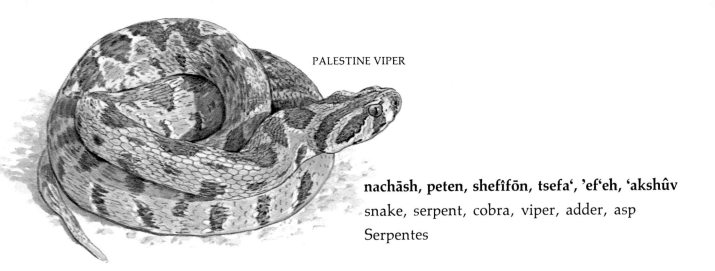

PALESTINE VIPER

nachāsh, peten, shefîfōn, tsefaʻ, ʼefʻeh, ʻakshûv

snake, serpent, cobra, viper, adder, asp

Serpentes

There are more than twenty references to snakes in the Bible, beginning with the story of the fall of man:

> Now the serpent was more subtle than any beast of the field which the Lord God had made. . . . And the Lord God said unto the serpent, Because thou hast done this, thou art cursed above all cattle, and above every beast of the field; upon thy belly shalt thou go, and dust shalt thou eat all the days of thy life: And I will put enmity between thee and the woman, and between thy seed and her seed; it shall bruise thy head, and thou shalt bruise his heel (Genesis 3:1,14-15).

Although enmity toward the snake goes back thousands of years, it has not been regarded with hate and fear everywhere. In ancient Egypt it signified life, health, and immortality.

After the Israelites destroyed the Canaanites, they were plagued with snakes:

> Then the Lord sent fiery serpents among the people, and they bit the people, so that many people of Israel died. And the people came to Moses, and said, We have sinned, for we have spoken against the Lord, and against you; pray to the Lord, that he take away the serpents from us. So Moses prayed for the people. . . . So Moses made a bronze serpent and set it on a pole; and if a serpent bit any man, he would look at the bronze serpent and live (Numbers 21:6-7,9; Revised Standard Version).

In the days of Hezekiah, this bronze serpent was destroyed:

> He removed the high places, and broke the pillars. . . .
> And he broke in pieces the bronze serpent that Moses had made, for until those days the people of Israel had burned incense to it . . .
> (II Kings 18:4; Revised Standard Version).

Seven Hebrew words appearing in the Bible have been translated, rather indiscriminately, as different kinds of snakes. The word nāchāsh is generic, denoting no particular species, although it seems to refer to poisonous snakes only. With the exception of the cobra, the only fully poisonous snakes found in the Holy Land are vipers. In English translations, adder, which is synonymous with viper, is often used. The Egyptian cobra (*Naja haje*) is commonly used by snake charmers, while the desert cobra (*Walterinnesia aegyptia*), found in Israel, is not.

> Their poison is like the poison of a serpent; they are like the deaf adder [peten] that stoppeth her ear; Which will not harken to the voice of charmers, charming never so wisely (Psalms 58:4-5).

A viper hidden along the path symbolized the tribe of Dan:

> Dan shall be a serpent by the way, an adder [shefîfōn] in the path, that biteth the horse heels, so that his rider shall fall backward (Genesis 49:17).

It has been suggested that the horned viper (*Cerastes cerastes*) was intended here, since that species has the habit of hiding itself in the sand.

Tsefa', is sometimes translated in the Authorized Version as cockatrice, a mythological creature, and sometimes as viper. The only deadly snake north of the desert in Israel is the Palestine viper (*Vipera palaestinae*).

> For, behold, I will send serpents, cockatrices [tsefa'] among you, which will not be charmed, and they shall bite you, saith the Lord (Jeremiah 8:17).

The sawscale or carpet viper (*Echis carinatus* or *E. colorata*), which occurs in the desert, may have been intended in the following passage:

> The burden of the beasts of the south: into the land of trouble and anguish, from whence come . . . the viper ['ef'eh] and fiery flying serpent (Isaiah 30:6).

Snakes are mentioned in comparison with the evils of wine:

> At the last it biteth like a serpent, and stingeth like an adder (Proverbs 23:32).

and in the prophecy of the peaceful kingdom to come:

> And the sucking child shall play on the hole of the asp, and the weaned child shall put his hand on the ˙ cockatrice den (Isaiah 11:8).

The 'akshûv is mentioned only once:

> They make their tongue sharp as a serpent's, and under their lips is the poison of vipers. Selah (Psalms 140:3; Revised Standard Version).

EGYPTIAN COBRA

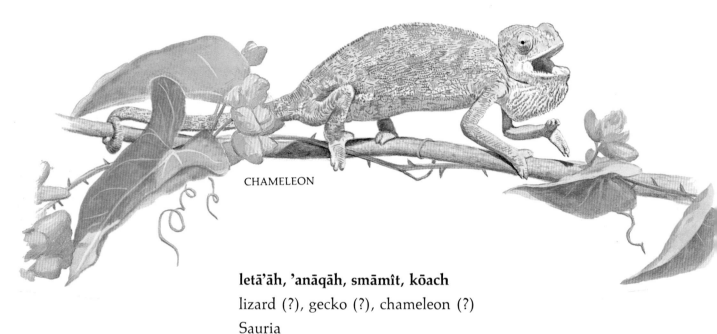

CHAMELEON

letā'āh, 'anāqāh, smāmît, kōach
lizard (?), gecko (?), chameleon (?)
Sauria

The word letā'āh, which means lizard in modern Hebrew, occurs only once, among unclean creeping animals in Leviticus 11:30. It has been translated as lizard and may be generic for the entire suborder. While many species of lizards occur in the Holy Land, the conspicuous agamas are most numerous and widespread. The identification of letā'āh remains uncertain.

'Anāqāh also is mentioned only once, and in the same verse. The Authorized Version translates it as ferret, which is not an inhabitant of the Holy Land; the Revised Standard Version gives gecko, which is more logical in the context. Possibly 'anāqāh referred to the large desert monitor (*Varanus grisens*), a lizard 4 feet long.

Smāmît, mentioned once, is translated in the Authorized Version as spider (see 'akbîsh); the Revised Standard Version and the Anchor Bible give lizard.

> The lizard [gecko, smāmît] can be caught in the hands, but it [makes its way] into royal palaces (Proverbs 30:28; Anchor Bible).

The Mediterranean house gecko (*Hemidactylus turcicus*) is extremely common.

The kōach, another unclean creeping animal (Leviticus 11:30) is translated as chameleon (*Chamaeleo chamaeleon*) in the Authorized Version. Tristram thought that this was the monitor lizard and that the tinshemet (see tinshemet) might be the chameleon. Neither identification can be verified.

STARRED LIZARD

MOORISH TORTOISE

tsāv
Moorish tortoise (*Testudo graeca*) (?); spiny-tailed lizard (*Uromastix aegyptiaca*) (?)

Tsāv appears only in the listing of unclean creeping things (Leviticus 11:29) and is translated as tortoise in the Authorized Version. It is thought by some to be the Arabic dabb, which is possibly the spiny-tailed lizard (*Uromastix aegyptiaca*).

LAUGHING FROG

AMPHIBIANS

tsefardē'a
laughing frog
Rana ridibunda

Tsefardē'a occurs only in the description of the plague sent upon Egypt and in passages referring to that event.

And the Lord spake unto Moses, Go unto Pharaoh, and say unto him, Thus saith the Lord, Let my people go, that they may serve me.
And if thou refuse to let them go, behold, I will smite all thy borders with frogs:
And the river shall bring forth frogs abundantly, which shall go up and come into thine house, and into thy bedchamber, and upon thy bed, and into the house of thy servants, and upon thy people, and into thine ovens, and into thy kneading troughs:
And the frogs shall come up both on thee, and upon thy people, and upon all thy servants.
And the Lord spake unto Moses, Say unto Aaron, Stretch forth thine hand with thy rod over the streams, over the rivers, and over the ponds, and cause frogs to come up upon the land of Egypt.
And Aaron stretched out his hand over the waters of Egypt; and the frogs came up, and covered the land of Egypt. . . .
Then Pharaoh called for Moses and Aaron, and said, Intreat the Lord, that he may take away the frogs from me, and from my people; and I will let the people go, that they may do sacrifice unto the Lord.
And Moses said unto Pharaoh, Glory over me: when shall I intreat for thee, and for thy servants, and for thy people, to destroy the frogs from thee and thy houses, that they may remain in the river only?
And he said, To morrow. And he said, Be it according to thy word: that thou mayest know that there is none like unto the Lord our God.
And the frogs shall depart from thee, and from thy houses, and from thy servants, and from thy people; they shall remain in the river only.
And Moses and Aaron went out from Pharaoh: and Moses cried unto the Lord because of the frogs which he had brought against Pharaoh.
And the Lord did according to the word of Moses; and the frogs died out of the houses, out of the villages, and out of the fields.
And they gathered them together upon heaps: and the land stank (Exodus 8:1-6, 8-14).

Both the laughing frog, which is edible, and the tree frog (*Hyla arborea savignyi*) are common in Israel.

FISH

dag
fish
Piscedae

In the Bible, fish are not identified by species but are distinguished according to those that are edible or inedible by Mosaic law (Leviticus 11:9-12; Deuteronomy 14:9-10). Those with fins and scales were permitted as food; those without fins or scales were unclean and forbidden. Examples are the St. Peters fish (*Tilapia galilea*), which is permitted, and the catfish (*Clarias lazera*) and eel (*Anguillula vulgaris*), which are not.

Fishing was done with dragnets (Isaiah 19:8; Matthew 13:47-48); by casting nets (Matthew 4:18); by hook and line (Isaiah 19:8); (Matthew 17:27); by spearing (Job 41:7). Fish were marketed in Jerusalem (Nehemiah 13:16). The complete absence of fish in the Dead Sea was noted by Ezekiel, who prophesied a change:

> And it shall come to pass that . . . there shall be a very great multitude of fish. . . .
> And it shall come to pass, that the fishers shall stand upon it from En-gedi even unto En-eglaim;
> they shall be a place to spread forth nets; their fish shall be according to their kinds,
> as the fish of the great sea, exceeding many (Ezekiel 47:9-10).

The legend of Jonah and the "great fish" is one of the great fish stories of all time:

> Now the Lord had prepared a great fish to swallow up Jonah. And Jonah was in the belly
> of the fish three days and three nights. . . .
> And the Lord spake unto the fish, and it vomited out Jonah upon the dry land
> (Jonah 1:17; 2:10).

Those who try to authenticate the story will be hard-pressed to find a fish that is big enough to swallow a man whole. There is a record that a sperm whale (a mammal) swallowed a shark nearly 10 feet long intact. There are many records of man-eating sharks, but they lacerate their prey. The sperm whale is rare off the coast of Israel (see tannîn).

ST. PETER'S FISH   COMMON EEL   CATFISH

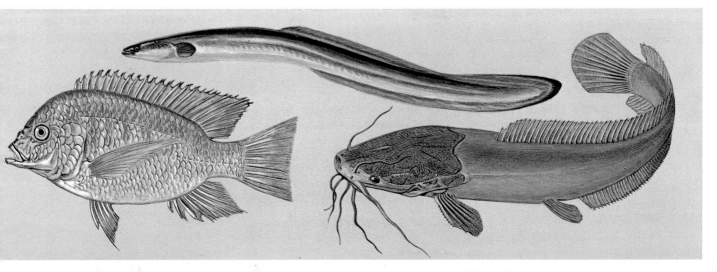

MIGRATORY LOCUST

INSECTS

chāgāv, 'arbeh, yeleq, chāsîl, gāzām, sol'ām, chargōl, tselātsal
grasshopper, locust, beetle (?), caterpillar (?), cankerworm (?), palmerworm (?)
Orthoptera

The grasshopper or locust appears in the Bible more often than any other insect and played an important part in the rural regions of the Middle East. When the locusts swarm, they destroy nearly every edible thing in sight. This was probably the reason for permission to eat the locust itself. The many different names, perhaps synonymous or referring to larval stages, have been translated as beetle, caterpillar, and so forth.

> Even these of them ye may eat; the locust ['arbeh] after his kind, and the bald locust [sol'ām] after his kind, and the beetle [chargōl] after his kind, and the grasshopper [chāgāv] after his kind (Leviticus 11:22).
>
> That which the palmerworm [gāzām] hath left hath the locust ['arbeh] eaten; and that which the locust hath left hath the cankerworm [yeleq] eaten; and that which the cankerworm hath left, hath the caterpillar [chāsîl] eaten (Joel 1:4).

LARVAL STAGES

All thy trees and fruit of thy land shall the locust [tselātsal] consume (Deuteronomy 28:42).

The heliothermal behavior of grasshoppers was noticed by the prophet Nahum:

Thy crowned are as the locusts ['arbeh] and thy captains as the great grasshoppers [chāgāv] which camp in the hedges in the cold day, but when the sun ariseth they flee away and their place is not known where they are (Nahum 3:17).

The migratory desert locust (*Schistocerca gregaria*) is unmistakably described in the following passage:

. . . when it was morning, the east wind brought the locusts. . . .
For they covered the face of the whole earth, so that the land was darkened; and they did eat every herb of the land, and all the fruit of the trees which the hail had left:
and there remained not any green thing in the trees, or in the herbs of the field,
through all the land of Egypt (Exodus 10:13,15).

The enemies of Israel were compared to locust hordes:

And they encamped against them, and destroyed the increase of the earth, till thou come unto Gaza, and left no sustenance for Israel, neither sheep, nor ox, nor ass.
For they came up with their cattle and their tents, and they came as grasshoppers for multitude; for both they and their camels were without number; and they entered into the land to destroy it (Judges 6:4-5).

75

'āsh, sās
clothes moth and larvae
Tineola biselliella, Tinea pellionella

The ancients evidently suffered from the depredations of the wool-eating larvae of clothes moths, which are still widespread pests. Dermestid beetle larvae also eat wool.

> For the moth ['āsh] shall eat them up like a garment; and the worm (sās) shall eat them like wool . . . (Isaiah 51:8).

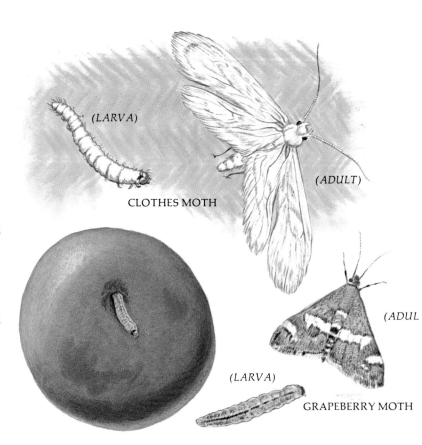

CLOTHES MOTH

(LARVA)

(ADULT)

(ADUL

(LARVA)

GRAPEBERRY MOTH

tola' (*pl.*, tôlā'îm), tôla'at (fem.), tôlē'ah, rimmāh
larvae of beetles, moths, and flies

Both tôlā'îm and rimmāh are usually translated as worms but refer to the wormlike larvae of various insects. See tôla'at shānî; sās.

The larvae of the grape-berry moth (*Polychrosis betrana*) have been known to damage as much as 80 percent of a crop of wine grapes. In addition, the leaf and flower buds of the vine are eaten by the larvae of the grapevine smoky moth (*Antispilla rivillei*), thereby reducing the yield.

> Thou shalt plant vineyards, and dress them, but shalt neither drink of the wine, nor gather the grapes; for the worms (tôlā'îm) shall eat them (Deuteronomy 28:39).

The bluebottle fly maggot (*Calliphora erythrocephala*) and the flesh fly maggot (*Sarcophaga* species) lay their eggs on carcasses, and the larvae emerge and feed on the decaying tissue. In the following passage tôlā'îm, although translated as worms, refers to these larvae:

And they shall go forth, and look upon the carcasses of the men that have transgressed against me: for their worms [tôlā'îm] shall not die, neither shall their fire be quenched . . . (Isaiah 66:24).

Other passages quite obviously referring to the same maggots use the Hebrew word rimmāh.

They shall lie down alike in the dust, and the worms [rimmāh] shall cover them (Job 21:26).

The womb shall forget him; the worm [rimmāh] shall feed sweetly on him; he shall be no more remembered . . . (Job 24:20).

tôla'at shānî

dye from cochineal scale insect
(*Kermes nahalaii*, *Kermes greeni*,
Kermes biblicus)

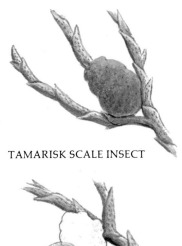

TAMARISK SCALE INSECT

Several species of cochineal scale insects, which yield carmine dye, are found on oaks in northern Israel and nearby Syria. In modern Hebrew tôla'at shānî means crimson larva (see also tola'.)

CARMESIN SCALE INSECT

(FEMALE EXCRETES DROPS OF HONEYDEW)

Come now, and let us reason together, saith the Lord: though your sins be as scarlet, they shall be as white as snow; though they be red like crimson, they shall be as wool (Isaiah 1:18).

mān

manna (scale insect excretion?)

(DRIED GRAINS OF EXCRETION)

Mān, translated as manna, is the name given the miraculous bread from heaven.

. . . Behold, I will rain bread from heaven for you. . . .
And when the dew that lay was gone up, behold, upon the face of the wilderness there lay a small round thing, as small as the hoar frost on the ground (Exodus 16:4,14).

It has been suggested that the idea of manna may have originated in the fact that there are scale insects (*Trabutina mannipara* and *Najococcus serpentinus*) living on desert tamarisks, which excrete drops of sweet fluid that dry and fall to the ground. The Bedouin collect and eat this. Unlike the manna of the Bible, however, it occurs in very small quantities.

HONEYBEE

devôrāh

Syrian honeybee

Apia mellifica syriaca

The honeybee was venerated by the Egyptians and was of great importance to the ancients as the major source of sweetening. Several references to the bee and its honey appear in the Bible.

> Butter and honey shall he eat, that he may know to refuse the evil,
> and choose the good (Isaiah 7:15).

The promised land, where bee-keeping was known, was described as "a land flowing with milk and honey" (Exodus 13:5). Although there is no mention of bee-keeping in the Old Testament, honey was one of the delicacies sent to Egypt by Jacob and it was supplied to the market at Tyre by Judah. Samson found "a swarm of bees and honey" in the carcass of a lion which he had killed (Judges 14:8).

The ferocity of bees when disturbed is also mentioned:

> And the Amorites, which dwelt in that mountain, came out against you, and
> chased you, as bees do, and destroyed you in Seir, even unto Hormah
> (Deuteronomy 1:44).

> And it shall come to pass in that day, that the Lord shall hiss . . .
> for the bee that is in the land of Assyria (Isaiah 7:18).

tsir'āh

oriental wasp (*Vespa orientalis*) (?)

Tsir'āh has been translated as hornet or wasp. If this is correct, the term may be generic for social wasps. Among those that inhabit Israel, the large oriental wasp is both common and conspicuous for its bright coloring. Its sting is very painful, and anyone who disturbs these wasps at their nest is attacked and driven away.

> Moreover the Lord thy God will send the hornet
> among them [the Canaanites], until they that
> are left, and hide themselves from thee,
> be destroyed (Deuteronomy 7:20).

ORIENTAL WASP

nemālāh

ant

Formicidae

Nemālāh clearly means the ant and may be generic
for the more than 100 species that inhabit Israel.
The activity of the ant is alluded to as an example
of foresight and is mentioned several times in
parables:

> Go to the ant, thou sluggard; consider
> her ways, and be wise:
> Which having no guide, overseer, or ruler,
> Provideth her meat in the summer and
> gathereth her food in the harvest
> (Proverbs 6:6-8).

> There be four things which are little upon
> the earth, but they are exceeding wise:
> The ants are a people not strong, yet they
> prepare their meat in the summer
> (Proverbs 30:24-25).

These passages seem most applicable to the grain-
collecting ants of the genus *Messor*, particularly
M. semirufus, which is perhaps the most common
species. The references are to the mass collecting
of grains in the summer and autumn by these ants.
Some travel more than 150 yards to collect seeds.
When the seeds stored in the upper chambers of the
nest become moist they are brought to the surface
to be dried in heaps. Ants are abundant in Israel,
as any housewife can testify.

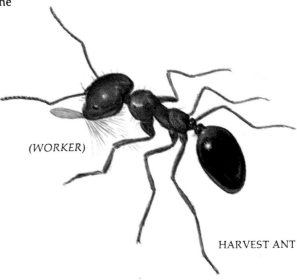

(WORKER)

HARVEST ANT

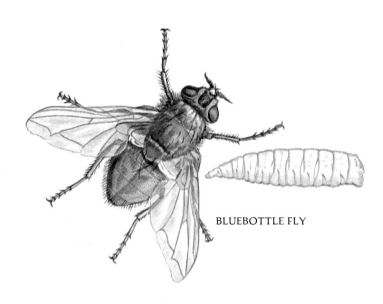

BLUEBOTTLE FLY

zvûv, ʻārōv

flies and gnats

Diptera

When the plague of flies brought upon Egypt is described, the word used is ʻārōv. This may be a generic term for small dipterous insects, especially those that bite, including mosquitoes, gnats, and midges, as well as flies.

> Else, if thou wilt not let my people go, behold, I will send swarms of flies upon thee, and upon thy servants, and upon thy people, and into thy houses: and the houses of the Egyptians shall be full of swarms of flies, and also the ground whereon they are (Exodus 8:21).

> He spake, and there came divers sorts of flies, and lice in all their coasts (Psalms 105:31).

> He sent divers sorts of flies among them, which devoured them . . . (Psalms 78:45).

In the following passage, the Hebrew word is zvûv.

> . . . the Lord shall hiss for the fly that is in the uttermost part of the rivers of Egypt (Isaiah 7:18).

In the New Testament the Greek word for gnat is used as a metaphor from the custom of straining wine before drinking:

> You blind guides, straining out a gnat and swallowing a camel! (Matthew 23:24; Revised Standard Version).

80

MALARIA MOSQUITO

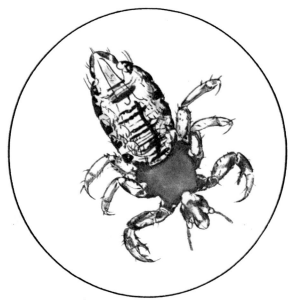

BODY LOUSE

kinnîm, kēn, kinnām

biting or sucking insect, louse (?), flea (?)
Mallophaga, Anoplura

Kinnîm are mentioned only in connection with the
Egyptian plague, and some authorities believe that
the term may be specific for the louse.

> And the Lord said unto Moses, Say unto
> Aaron, Stretch out thy rod, and smite
> the dust of the land, that it may become
> lice throughout all the land of Egypt.
> And they did so; for Aaron stretched out
> his hand with his rod, and smote the
> dust of the earth, and it became lice in
> man, and in beast; all the dust of land
> became lice throughout all the land of
> Egypt (Exodus 8:16-17).

> He spake and there came . . . lice in all
> their coasts (Psalms 105:31).

Gnats or mosquitoes have been suggested,
but these hatch in water and not dust. Flea is a
more likely alternative (see par'ōsh).

par'ōsh

flea (*Pulex irritans*) (?)
Siphonaptera, Pulcidae

Par'ōsh occurs twice in the
Old Testament and has been
translated as flea. Fleas are a great
pest to man and beast and,
together with lice, are responsible
for the transmission of disease
from rats and other animals to
humans. The biblical passages
suggest that the par'ōsh is an
insignificant creature.

After whom is the
King of Israel come
out? after whom dost
thou pursue? after a
dead dog, after a flea
(I Samuel 24:14).

Now therefore, let not
my blood fall to the
earth before the face
of the Lord: for the
king of Israel is come
out to seek a flea . . .
(I Samuel 26:20).

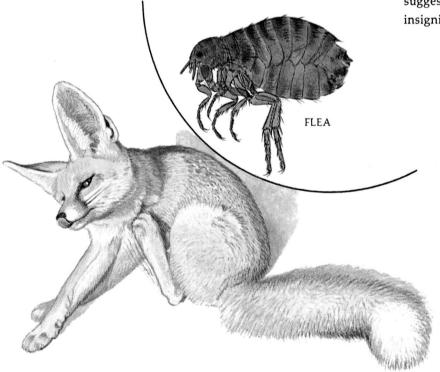

FLEA

ARACHNIDS

'aqrāv

scorpion

Scorpiones

The scorpion appears in the Bible as a symbol of desolation:

> Who led thee through that great and terrible wilderness,
> wherein were fiery serpents, and scorpions, and drought . . .
> (Deuteronomy 8:15).

and as a divine scourge:

> . . . their torment was as the torment of a scorpion, when he
> striketh a man (Revelation 9:5).

Jesus, sending his apostles out to work miracles, used the words:

> Behold, I give unto you power to tread on serpents and scorpions,
> and over all the power of the enemy: and nothing shall by any
> means hurt you (Luke 10:19).

The sting of a scorpion is painful but not dangerous to human
adults, although it may be fatal to young children. Scorpions are widespread
and common in the Holy Land but owing to their nocturnal habits are seldom
seen. Many species have been named, but the most common are the yellow
scorpion *Buthus questriatus* and the black *B. judaicus*.

SCORPION

SPIDER WEB

'akbîsh

spiders
Araneidae

The word 'akbîsh is used in
connection with the spider's web
in Job 8:14 and Isaiah 59:5,6. The
word smāmît, which occurs only
once (Proverbs 30:28) is also translated in the Authorized Version
as spider, but modern translations
give lizard (see smāmît).

Hundreds of species of
spiders inhabit the Holy Land; it is
not unlikely that there was one
generic term for all.

MALMIGNATTE (SPIDER)

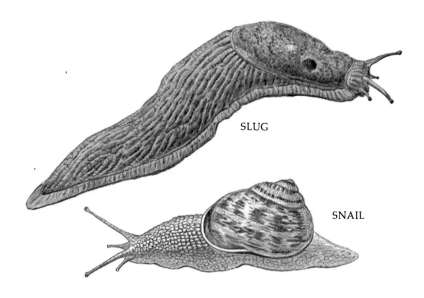

SLUG

SNAIL

MOLLUSKS

shabbelûl, chōmet (?)

snail, slug

Gastropoda

Shabbelûl refers to a snail or slug:

> As a snail which melteth, let every one of them
> pass away (Psalms 58:8).

The passage may allude to the abundant slime secreted by the slug, or to the effect of salt upon it. The slug is closely related to the land snail, but its shell is only rudimentary.

Chōmet, which appears in the listing of unclean creeping things (Leviticus 11:30), is translated as snail in the Authorized Version and as sand lizard in the Revised Standard Version; the identification is questionable.

shichēlet

operculum of conch or wing shell (*Strombus*)(?)

There are two references to shichēlet in the Bible, once as an ingredient of the incense used in religious services (Exodus 30:34; translated as onycha) and, in the Apocrypha, as a very fragrant substance. Onycha was obtained from a small shell (operculum) on the foot of many mollusks that serves to close entrance to the main shell. Many species of conchs occur in the Red Sea and a few in the Mediterranean. In Sinai the Bedouin eat the conch or use it for bait.

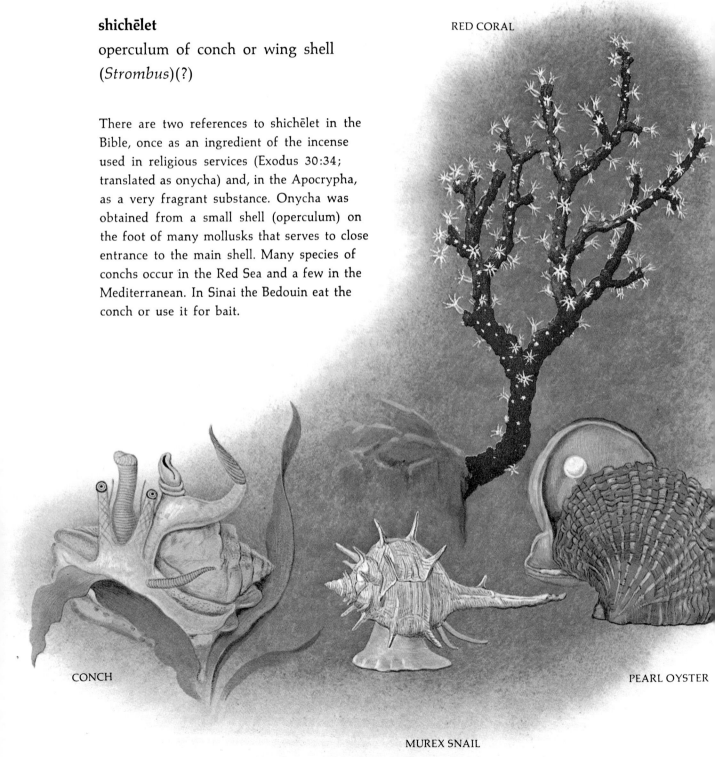

RED CORAL

CONCH

PEARL OYSTER

MUREX SNAIL

'argāmān, tekēlet

Tyrian purple, blue dye from mollusks
Murex brandaris, or *Murex trunculus*

The words 'argāmān and tekēlet appear in the Bible as colors of the cloth
to be used as curtains for the Tabernacle (Exodus 26:36), and as objects of
commerce (Ezekiel 27:7,16). Purple and blue dyes were extracted from the
adrectal gland of certain species of gastropod mollusks found in the
Mediterranean. They were an important article of trade in ancient times.

gābîsh, penînîm

pearls (?); pearl oyster (*Avicula, Pinctada
margaritifera*) (?)

In Job 28:18 gābîsh is translated as pearls in the Authorized Version and
penînîm as rubies; in the Revised Standard Version gābîsh is given as
crystal and penînîm as pearls, which is the meaning of that word in modern
Hebrew. This doubtful passage is the only reference to pearls in the
Old Testament, although the New Testament contains several.
   Pearls are produced when layers of calcium carbonate form around a
foreign body in the mantle of the oyster. The pearl oyster is abundant in the
Persian Gulf and Red Sea.

ANTHOZOANS

rā'môt

coral (Anthozoa, Hydrozoa) (?)

Coral is included by virtue of a single reference to it among the commodities
listed as imported from Syria (Ezekiel 27:16). Many exquisite forms of
reef-forming corals abound in the Red Sea. The species used for jewelry occur
in the Mediterranean, but not near the Levantine coast.

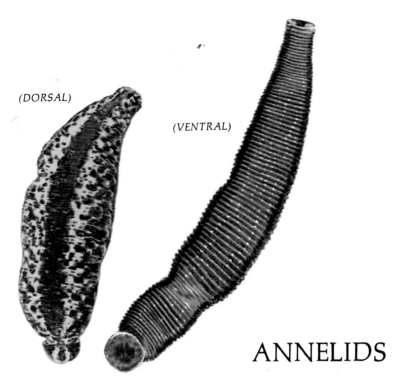

(DORSAL)

(VENTRAL)

MEDICINAL LEECH

ANNELIDS

'alûqāh

leech (limnic worm)

Hirudinae

The 'alûqāh is mentioned only once in the Bible:

> The leech has two daughters—Give! Give! . . .
> (Proverbs 30:15; Anchor Bible).

The name comes from the root 'LQ, meaning "to cling to"; and words meaning leech are used for it in the Septuagint and Vulgate. It may denote some species of leech or may be a generic term. Some translators have thought that 'alûqāh referred to the vampire-bat, but that species does not occur in the Old World. In Arabic the leech is called 'alaq, and many springs are named Bir el 'Aluqat. The leeches *Limnatis nilotica* and *Haemopsis sanguisuga* prey on small water animals and sometimes enter the throats of larger animals and people, causing intense discomfort or worse. The medicinal leech (*Hiruda medicinalis*), used to reduce swellings, is found in northern Israel.

zōchalē
earthworm (Lumbricidae) (?)

Most of the references to worms in English translations of the Bible should read larvae (see tôla'). However, there is one passage where the earthworm may indeed have been intended, and in this case the Hebrew word is zōchalē.

> They shall lick the dust like a serpent, they shall move out of their holes like worms of the earth . . . (Micah 7:17).

In biblical times, much of the land was forested. The overgrazing which degraded and destroyed most of the forests and led to widespread soil erosion incidentally destroyed much of the habitat of the earthworm.

The word zōchalē also occurs in Deuteronomy 32:24, but there a reference to venom suggests that a snake is meant. The identification remains doubtful.

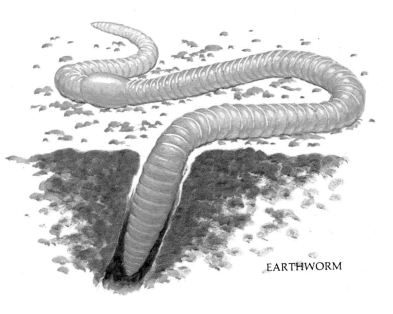

EARTHWORM

Animals figure prominently in many primitive and ancient religions. The numerous references to them in the Bible provide not only a clue to many of the customs and beliefs of the early Hebrews, but the first written record of the zoology of the region. It is hoped that this study will contribute toward a better understanding of those passages that allude to animals and make for more vivid and enjoyable reading.

SELECTED BIBLIOGRAPHY

INDEX

SELECTED BIBLIOGRAPHY

BIBLES

Authorized (King James) Version.
Revised Standard Version.
The Anchor Bible. Edited by W. F. Albright and D. N. Freedman. New York: Doubleday, 1964–.
The Holy Bible. Facsimile series no. 5. London: Oxford University Press.
Hebrew Bible.

DICTIONARIES, CONCORDANCE

Bible Dictionary. Edited by W. Smith. Philadelphia: Winston, 1884.
A Concise Hebrew and Aramaic Lexicon of the Old Testament. Translated by William L. Holladay. Grand Rapids, Mich.: Eerdmans, 1972.
Dictionary of the Bible. Edited by James Hastings. Rev. ed. New York: Charles Scribner's Sons, 1963.
Fuerstio, J. *Concordantiae Hebraicae.* Leipzig: Jonas Verleger, 1932.

NATURAL HISTORY

Bare, Garland. *Plants and Animals of the Bible: A Translator's Workbook.* United Bible Societies, 1969.
Bodenheimer, F. S. *Animal and Man in Bible Lands.* New York: Humanities Press, 1960.
Cansdale, G. S. *Animals of Bible Lands.* Paternoster Press.
Harper, F. *Extinct and Vanishing Mammals of the Old World.* American Committee for Wild Life Protection, 1945.
Harrison, D. L. *Mammals of Arabia.* London: Ernest Benn, 1968.
Lydekker, R. *The Royal Natural History.* New York: Frederick Warne, 1893–94.
Meinertzhagen, R. *Birds of Arabia.* London: Oliver and Boyd, 1954.
Parmelee, Alice. *All the Birds of the Bible.* New York: Harper, 1959.
Pinney, *Animals in the Bible.* Philadelphia: Chilton, 1964.
Pope, Clifford H. *The Reptile World.* New York: Knopf, 1956.
Porter, G. S. *Birds of the Bible.* New York: Abingdon, 1909.
Tristram, H. B. *Natural History of the Bible.* London: Society for the Promotion of Christian Knowledge, 1898.
Walker, E. P. *Mammals of the World.* Baltimore: Johns Hopkins University Press, 1964.
Wood, J. G. *Wild Animals of the Bible.* London: Longmans, 1887.
Zeuner, F. E. *History of Domesticated Animals.* New York: Harper & Row, 1963.

INDEX

ENGLISH NAMES

BIBLICAL HEBREW NAMES

'āgûr, 64
'akbār, 39
'akbîsh, 84
'akshûv, 68
'alûqāh, 88
'anāfāh, 44
'anāqāh, 70
'appô, 36
'aqrāv, 83
'arbeh, 74
'argāmān, 87
'arî, 18
'arnevet, 38
'ārôd, 24
'arōv, 80
'aryeh, 18
'āsh, 76
'atallef, 11
'atôn, 23
'ayil, 35
'ayir, 23
'ayit, 17
ayyāh, 50
'ayyāl, 28
bāqār, 27
barburîm 'abusîm, 48
bat ya'anāh, 46
behēmôt, 33
bēker, 32
bikrāh, 32
chafarfērôth, 38
chāgāv, 74
chamôr, 23
chargōl, 74
chasîdāh, 45
chāsîl, 74
chazîr, 25
chōled, 38
chōmet, 85
dag, 73
dāyāh, 50
devôrāh, 78
dîshôn, 31

dōv, 16
drôr, 64
dûkîfat, 65
'ef'eh, 68
'ēgel, 27
'ēz, 37
gābîsh, 87
gāmāl, 32
gāzām, 74
gedî, 37 ·
gôzāl, 60
gûr, 18
kārîm, 35
kefîr, 18
kelev, 12
kēn, 81
keves, 35
kinnām, 81
kinnîm, 81
kivsāh, 35
kōach, 70
kôs, 54
lāvî', 18
layish, 18
letā'āh, 70
lîlît, 54
livyātān, 66
mān, 77
nāchāsh, 68
nāmēr, 20
nemālāh, 79
nesher, 50
nēts, 53
'ôf, 42
'ōrēv, 62
'oznîyyāh, 53
par, 27
pārāh, 27
par'ōsh, 82
penînîm, 87
pere', 24
pered, 23
peres, 52

peten, 68
qā'at, 43
qippōd, 43
qippôz, 54
qōf, 10
qōrē, 56
rāchām, 50
rā'môt, 87
re'ēm, 26
rekesh, 22
rimmāh, 76
śā'îr, 37
sās, 76
shabbelûl, 85
shachaf, 63
shachal, 18
shāfān, 21
shālāk, 48
shefîfōn, 68
shichēlet, 86
shôr, 27
shû'āl, 15
sîs, 64
slāv, 57
smāmît, 70
sol'ām, 74
sûs, 22
tachash, 40
tachmās, 59
tan, 14
tannîn, 41
tayish, 37
tekēlet, 87
te'ô, 30
tinshemet, 54
tola', 76
tôla'at, 76
tôla'at shānî, 77
tôlē'āh, 76
tôr, 61
tsāfîr, 37
tsāv, 71
tsefa', 68

tsefardē'a, 72
tselātsal, 74
tsemed, 27
tsippôr, 42
tsir'āh, 78
tsō'n, 35
tsvî, 29
tukkî, 59
yachmûr, 31
yā'ēl, 36
yā'ēn, 46
yanshûf, 54
yeleq, 74
yônāh, 60
ze'ēv, 13
zemer, 35
zōchalē, 89
zvûv, 80

ABOUT THE AUTHOR

Walter W. Ferguson has exhibited his paintings in
museums in the United States and has had several one-man
shows. In addition to portraying the people of many
countries, he has specialized in painting birds and other
animals. He has done illustrations for *Audubon* and *The
New York Times* and has provided pictures for numerous
books. Born in New York City in 1930, he now lives in
Israel.